Libraries
and the Life of the Mind
in America

Libraries
and the Life of the Mind
in America

Addresses Delivered
at the Centennial Celebration of the
American Library Association

AMERICAN LIBRARY ASSOCIATION
Chicago 1977

Library of Congress Cataloging in Publication Data

Main entry under title:
Libraries and the life of the mind in America.
    Lectures given in commemoration of the centennial anniversary of the American Library Association.
    1. Libraries — United States — Addresses, essays, lectures. I. American Library Association.
Z731.L544   021′.00973   77-3288
ISBN 0-8389-0238-3

Printed in the United States of America

CONTENTS

INTRODUCTION

When the American Library Association began formulating plans for its Centennial, a variety of ideas was expressed. Not being an association with much of an appreciation for its past, ALA was unlikely to spend much of its time reveling in the glories that were or in the grandeur that was not. The Association has always been pragmatic in the American sense. No one exemplifies the pragmatism of American librarianship better than the redoubtable Melvil Dewey, whose interests encompassed many activities of which scholarship was perhaps the least important. He wanted a library world standardized, organized, and administered in line with the efficiency of American business. Many of ALA's subsequent activities—from indexing to cataloging, from administration to library education—reflect this Dewey-eyed view.

Yet at the same time that ALA has been pragmatic, the Association has also taken pride in the fact that its promotion of libraries was allied with that fundamental premise of a democratic society as expressed by Thomas Jefferson: no society could be ignorant and free. Thus the first and only charter of the American Library Association, adopted in 1879 and amended only once (1942), declares that certain individuals have associated themselves with the "intention of forming a corporation under the name of the American Library Association for the purpose of promoting the library interests of the country by exchanging views, reaching conclusions, and inducing cooperation in all departments of bibliothecal science and economy; by disposing the public mind to the founding and improving of libraries; and by cultivating good will among its own members. . . ." To this statement of purpose the Association added an international dimension in 1942 by substituting after the phrase "promoting library interests" the words "throughout the world" in place of the words "of the country." This broader world view came at a time when America was locked in battle with the forces of tyranny beyond its borders, but the change was really a recognition of a fact that already had existed for some time. That it would be an ideal rather than a reality did not take away from its fundamental importance. The American Library Association is committed to the broadest possible expansion of libraries and to the most inclusive membership as an educational and professional association. To paraphrase President Carter's campaign rhetoric, "ALA loves everybody" who wants to promote library interests throughout the world.

Despite our not being noted for our historical consciousness, some members thought that our conference celebration ought at least recognize the relationship between libraries and American history, especially in the year of ALA's Centennial and of America's Bicentennial. There was no intention that the series be pure nostalgia, but our celebration surely provided an occasion for looking at the past as a means of improving the present and the future. In 1974, when the San Francisco Conference Planning Committee and I were considering the program for 1975, one of our most articulate members, Kathleen Molz, suggested a two-year series of lectures by distinguished scholars who would discuss the development of libraries and their influence upon the American mind. Ms. Molz even gave the series a title, "Libraries and the Life of the Mind in America," which she admitted having borrowed from a book by the late historian Perry Miller, *The Life of the Mind in America* (1965). She thought that there were a number of topics which could deal with this theme but doubted that anyone would agree wholly with the topics finally chosen. However, it was an idea well worth consideration and I discussed the matter with the incoming president, Allie Beth Martin, so that the program for the two years 1975 and 1976 could be coordinated. With the enthusiasm and idealism which always marked that vibrant personality, Ms. Martin immediately agreed to Ms. Molz's proposal. The ALA Executive Board subsequently approved a series of six lectures to be called "Libraries and the Life of the Mind in America."

"The Life of the Mind" series, as the lectures came to be known, was launched in San Francisco in 1975 when John Hope Franklin, John Matthews Manly Professor of History at the University of Chicago, delivered the opening lecture on "Libraries in a Pluralistic Society" to one of the largest audiences ever to attend a general session. In his lecture on June 29, 1975, Professor Franklin traced the attempts of cultural and educational institutions to serve a varied democratic society. One could not have asked for a better speaker to open the series. His balanced presentation recognized that librarians, perhaps more than others, have called attention to the contributions of various ethnic, racial, and national groups to our collective heritage, but that librarians have also often reflected the darker phases of American society. He noted that American librarians "have many reasons to be pleased with their contributions to the life of the mind in the United States," but he noted also that they could not rest on yesterday's laurels but must "address themselves to today's problems in a creative and forthright manner." In ending his lecture Franklin was positive about the potential of librarians "to create a social order of peace, purposefulness, and mutual respect such as we have never known before."

The Franklin lecture was followed on July 2 by "Libraries and the Freedom of Access to Information," delivered by Dan M. Lacy, Senior Vice-President of McGraw-Hill. Lacy's speech was not on intellectual freedom but on the importance of a democratic people's having the widest possible access to information. He focused on the fact that knowledge is power and that the history of access to information in this country reflects attempts to bring more individuals into touch with such power. The real change came after World War II when the G.I. Bill opened colleges for the masses and when three new developments—the paperback book, television, and the computer—facilitated access to information on a broad scale. By 1970 the national policy of the United States had been enunciated as access to information for all citizens. Implementation of that policy paused in the early seventies. The recent financial crises have blighted the earlier promise of the sixties that access to information would be "freed, enlarged, and enriched at every level of society." In this period of retrenchment librarians have looked to networks as a panacea, but Lacy warned us that networks are likely to serve chiefly the researcher and to do little for the normal day-to-day needs of users. Few librarians would disagree with his statement that the greatest limitation on access to information is "lack of adequately supported libraries." In concluding his remarks Lacy urged his audience to remember that knowledge is power and the "key to participation in the service of our society and in its rewards." He hoped we could recapture the fervor of our earlier convictions and be ready for new opportunities when the current economic depression is over.

The third lecture in the series on July 3, 1975, was given, at my insistence, by Kathleen Molz and bore the title "Libraries and the Development and Future of Tax Support." Following the lead of Franklin and Lacy, who had both treated the philosophical bases of libraries and their service to diverse communities, Ms. Molz concentrated upon the long involvement of librarians in the legislative process—our successes, our failures, and our stance for the future. From our history she traced the contradictions and ambivalences about tax support, but, more important, she highlighted the two very differing goals for which librarians have sought tax support: bibliographical control and the spread of literacy and education for the masses. These two goals have created a dichotomy for academic and public librarians that has been reflected in the approach of ALA to the problem of tax support. The question for the federal government has been how to equalize resources and services to achieve the goal of equal educational opportunity for all. Ms. Molz suggested that the novelty of the new National Commission on Libraries and Information Science national plan would be the placing within a single context the dual philosophies of the profession and combining within a single service ideal the disparate aims of the public and academic librarian. For the future she recommended a client-centered not an institution-centered approach to federal policy makers, a greater cohesion of ALA's position, and more concern with policy research.

Although it had never occurred to this writer that he would ultimately be directly involved in all six lectures, the tragic illness and subsequent death of Ms. Martin made that necessary. Before her death on April 11, 1976, President Martin had already selected the speakers for the 1976 series. We had worked together closely in securing speakers who would meet the high standards Ms. Molz had in mind when the Life of the Mind series was first suggested. Ms. Martin would have been pleased with the high caliber of the 1976 lectures, as she would also have been pleased with the appearance of this volume.

At the opening general session of ALA's Centennial Conference in Chicago on July 19, 1976, Herman Liebaers, Grand Marshal to the Court of Belgium and President of the International Federation of Library Associations, 1969–74, presented "The Impact of American and European Librarianship Upon Each Other." His lecture was, as he noted, a personal one based on experience of the past twenty-five years. Liebaers traced ALA's long involvement with IFLA and the difficulties inherent in a relationship where one set of librarians relies heavily on their governments and the other on their professional associations. That cooperation on the international scene is both essential and difficult Liebaers acknowledged. He used the cases of UNISIST, "phony from the beginning," and Universal Bibliographical Control, "a world-wide system for control and exchange of bibliographical information," to illustrate the difference between unreality and reality in international library cooperation. Since World War II, ALA has been committed to international cooperation through the words of its charter but that emphasis has waned in recent years. Liebaers hoped that it will be strengthened, for the benefit of ALA and IFLA, in years immediately ahead.

Liebaers was followed on July 21 by the distinguished civil liberties lawyer, Harriet Pilpel, who paid tribute to ALA's long fight for intellectual freedom in her "Libraries and the First Amendment." Ms. Pilpel discussed the change in librarians' attitudes toward censorship in the last century and pointed out the change in subject matter which has been the object of censorship battles. Using the topics religion, race, sex, violence, and politics ("RSVP"), she elucidated her major points with examples from her experience in defending first amendment rights. The battleground shifts. Ms. Pilpel noted that sex and violence are major concerns today but that there is a rising concern among some anti-censorship individuals toward censorship of racist, sexist, and religious stereotypes. Ultimately, though, she came down on what she called "neutral principles," that is, "that all ideas and depictions should be welcome in a free marketplace of thought." In line with this principle she found the ALA's stand on censorship admirable: that the "criteria for content should be neutral, and no book should be censored on RSVP grounds. . . ." An addendum prepared after the speech was given quotes passages from a decision of the U.S. Court of Appeals for the Sixth Circuit concerning the selection of books for high school texts and for libraries.

Concluding the series was the new Librarian of Congress, Daniel J. Boorstin, who spoke on "The Indivisible Community" on July 22, 1976. In a high point of the conference, Boorstin was introduced by one of ALA's elder statesmen, Keyes D. Metcalf, retired librarian of Harvard University, who gave a vignette of the Librarians of Congress in this century, all of whom he had known personally. Metcalf's introduction was such a gem of brevity and wit that there was common agreement it should be included here.

Boorstin's lecture reminded us that public libraries are currently in limbo. Having moved into novel, intermediate roles, they nonetheless suffer from oblivion or neglect. Part of the problem is their derivative nature and part, the conflicts of purpose between preservation and diffusion of knowledge, between instruction and entertainment. Yet Boorstin believed that we can bring our public libraries out of limbo if we recall the importance of three principled motives that attended their emergence one hundred years ago: self-help, autonomy, and community. In an Age of Broadcasting, which has democratized experience, libraries can provide "escape from the limitations of this broadcast world." He provided thoughtful suggestions not only for the unique role of libraries but also for ways to enlist the aid of radio and television as allies of the book. In concluding his lecture Boorstin reminded his audience that the library is "par excellence a place of community, for there we share the spiritual wealth of all mankind." He pledged the fellowship of the Library of Congress in strengthening and improving libraries for the exploring spirit.

The Life of the Mind lectures were well received by large and enthusiastic audiences. Many individuals have since commented that the series did indeed achieve its original laudable aim of focusing on the contributions libraries and librarians have made to the evolution of the life of the mind in America. As I have re-read the lectures I have been impressed once more with their substance and with their continuing usefulness for the library profession. As many individuals have sought copies of the speeches, it is a pleasure for ALA to present the entire series in permanent form for the benefit of a wider audience.

For the support of these lectures ALA is indebted to the Encyclopaedia Britannica Incorporated, Field Enterprises Educational Corporation, the Grolier Educational Corporation, and the H. W. Wilson Company. We are grateful to these friends of librarians for their continued encouragement and support.

EDWARD G. HOLLEY, *Dean*
School of Library Science
University of North Carolina at Chapel Hill,
and *Past President,*
American Library Association

February 16, 1977

John Hope Franklin

John Matthews Manly Distinguished Service Professor of History
the University of Chicago

Professor Franklin has taught at many institutions in the
United States and other countries, among them Howard
University (1947–56) and Brooklyn College, where he
held the Chair in History (1956–64).
He has received many honorary degrees in recognition of
his work, which has led to a significant reassessment of
the role of black Americans in the nation's history. One of
his best-known books is *From Slavery to Freedom*, first
published in 1947 and now in its fourth edition. He has
served on the Editorial Board of the *Journal of Negro History*
and from 1973 to 1976 was President of the United
Chapters of Phi Beta Kappa. He is author of *Racial Equality in America* and, with John Caughey and
Ernest May, of *Land of the Free*.

LIBRARIES IN A PLURALISTIC SOCIETY

ONE WOULD BE hard pressed to find, anywhere on the face of this earth, a population more diverse in race, religion, and national origins than the people who make up the population of the United States. And this was true almost from the beginning. By the end of the first century of the existence of the English colonies, the governments were under the flag of the British government; but the people themselves represented many flags, many religions, many races. There were the Scandinavians, the Germans, the French, and the Dutch. In time, there would be peoples from numerous other European countries, from Africa, from Asia, and from Latin America. The babel of tongues would be more than matched by the diversity of religions, races, and national origins. Many had come quite voluntarily, with the hope that they would find in the New World all the good fortunes that had eluded them in the Old. Others had come most reluctantly, victims of slave traders and marauders who dumped them in the colonies and, later in the states, in exchange for whatever the market would bring. But rewards were held out for all: those who came voluntarily or involuntarily, if they were white, could look with optimism to the luxuriant rehabilitation of fame and fortune that awaited them. Those who came involuntarily, if they were black, were encouraged to wait patiently for their equally rich rewards—in the next world.

As early as the era of the American Revolution, the relative unimportance of background was emphasized by those who wanted to draw attention to the emerging Americanization of the former colonists. Perhaps the most eloquent observer of that period was that French student of American life, Hector St. Jean de Crèvecoeur. In seeking to describe the process of Americanization in 1782, he answered his own question, "What, then,

3

is the American this new man?" He said, "He is either an European, or the descendant of an European, hence that strange mixture of blood, which you will find in no other country. . . . He is an American who, leaving behind him all his ancient prejudices and manners, receives new ones from the new mode of the life he has embraced, the new government he obeys, and the new rank he holds. He becomes an American by being received in the broad lap of our great *Alma Mater*. Here individuals of all nations are melted into a new race of men, whose labours and posterity will one day cause great changes in the world."

This was one of the earliest and most clear-cut expressions of the notion of the pluralistic society in America, one that involved the creation of an entirely new mode of life that would complement but not entirely eradicate the ethnic backgrounds of those who were a part of the process. There were some glaring imprecisions and inaccuracies that would, in time, become a part of the lore or myth of the vaunted melting pot and would grossly misrepresent the crucial factor of race and even ethnicity in the pluralistic character of American life. It ignored the tenacity with which the Pennsylvania Dutch held on to their language, religion, and ways of life. It overlooked the way in which the Swedes of New Jersey remained Swedes and the manner in which the Huguenots of New York and Charleston held on to their own past as though it were the sole source of light and life. It described a process that in a distant day would gag at the notion that Irish Catholics could be assimilated on the broad lap of alma mater or that Asians could be seated on the basis of equality at the table of the Great American Feast.

By suggesting that only Europeans were involved in the process of becoming Americans, Crèvecoeur pointedly ruled out three quarters of a million blacks already in the country who, along with their progeny, would be regarded as ineligible to become Americans for at least another two centuries. To be sure, the number of persons of African descent would increase enormously over the next century, but the view of their ineligibility for Americanization would be very slow to change. It was beyond the conception of Crèvecoeur, as it was indeed beyond the conception of the Founding Fathers, that blacks, slave or free, could become true Americans, enjoying that fellowship in a common enterprise about which Crèvecoeur spoke so warmly. It was obvious that Americanization in the late eighteenth century was a precious commodity to be cherished and enjoyed only by a select group of persons of European descent.

Crèvecoeur was not alone in viewing the diversity of American society rather narrowly. Indeed, there were many Americans of the eighteenth and nineteenth centuries who made no apologies for their bigoted views that the true and only true Americans were those who belonged to their particular group. Thus, the Founding Fathers had difficulty in making up their minds about using Negro soldiers in the War for Independence; and only when the fortunes of the struggle against England took a decided turn for the worse did they finally conclude that blacks should be received in the Continental Army. In Philadelphia in November, 1787—two months after the writing of the Federal Constitution was completed—the trustees of the white St. George's Church pulled several Negroes from their knees during prayer because the Negroes had taken seats in the gallery several rows ahead of those to which they had been assigned. All of them left the church in a body and, as one of them later recalled, "they were no more plagued with us in the church." Some years later, in 1819, a Jewish immigrant in New York was chilled to hear a bystander refer to him and his companion as "more damned immigrants." A decade later there began a most scathing and multi-faceted attack on the Catholic church. Its principal recruits, the complaint said, were the Irish, the "very dregs" of the Old World social order; and its alleged doctrine of papal supremacy ran counter to the idea of the political and religious independence of the United States. The subsequent burning of convents and churches and the killing of Catholics themselves were indications of how deeply many Americans felt about religion and cultural differences for which they had a distaste and suspicion that bordered on paranoia.

This was hardly a congenial climate in which to nurture educational and cultural institutions that would serve all the people. And yet, efforts were made almost from the beginning to establish and maintain such institutions. The growth of schools and colleges during the colonial period and later indicated how the resources of a people could be channeled in a constructive direction. The establishment of Harvard College in 1636 was one of the first things that the colonists looked after once they had settled themselves in Massachusetts Bay. Almost a century later, in 1731, Benjamin Franklin noted the importance of books to the discussions that his beloved Junto held; and proceeding from the idea that the members might set up a library for their own use, he began to develop the first subscription library in English America.

There was a certain ambivalence, however, in the stance of those pioneers in the promotion of America's cultural growth. On the one hand they reflected a profound understanding of the importance of educational institutions and libraries in strengthening and promoting America's intellectual growth. No one expressed this understanding better than George Washington when he said in 1783, "The foundation of our Empire was not laid in a gloomy age of ignorance and superstition, but at an epoch when the rights of mankind were better understood and more clearly defined than at any former period. Researches of the human mind after social happiness have been carried to a great extent; the treasure of knowledge acquired by the labours of philosophers, sages, and legislators, thro' a long succession of years, are laid open for use, and their collected wisdom may be happily applied in the establishment of our forms of government."

On the other hand these efforts were almost invariably represented by and intended for special interest groups rather than the general public. Harvard College was founded to train ministers of a particular religious denomination. Benjamin Franklin's library was limited to fifty subscribers, and one searches in vain to find among that very small company any persons who represented interests that were, in any way, different from those of the founder. The mechanics and mercantile libraries of the 1820s and 1830s were essentially institutions to serve a special clientele; and when others benefited from such establishments, it was quite incidental to the main purpose for which they were founded. Only when libraries began to open their doors to persons who were required to pay a modest annual fee and only when New York and other communities began to support libraries from public funds did these crucial cultural institutions come within the reach of all or most of the citizens of the community.

This view of the importance of knowledge for the general public was well expressed by James DeBow in 1854, when he said, "Let us diffuse knowledge throughout the length and breadth of this great country, multiply the means of information,—send the schoolmaster into every home,—dot every hill with the schoolhouse and college,—let the press, without intermission, night and day, pour forth its steady stream of light,—foster science and the arts,—let the civilizing and Godlike influences of machinery uninterruptedly extend. Then will the future of our country open, boundless and great, beyond all example, beyond all compare, and countless ages bless its mission and acknowledge its glorious dominion."

DeBow was more eloquent in words than he was in deeds. At the time that he wrote these words, he was engaged in a fierce battle to preserve slavery; and he resorted to every conceivable means to advance the idea of the inferiority of Afro-Americans and of their utter lack of any capacity to benefit from the great educational and cultural heritage that was being developed in this country. And he was thus engaged at a time when the idea of public support for schools, colleges, and libraries was rapidly gaining ground. The efforts of DeBow and his numerous colleagues coincided, moreover, with the efforts of other groups to withhold cultural and educational opportunities from various other segments of American society.

In virtually every part of the country the influx of large numbers of immigrants in the 1820s and 1830s had galvanized the incipient suspicion and hostility of the original American stock toward the newcomers. Southerners tended to distrust immigrants because it was assumed that they were hostile to slavery, which was not always the case. Conservative Northerners disliked immigrants because some of them subscribed to various forms of social experimentation, including utopian socialism. Religious fundamentalists were alarmed by their presence because of their toleration of alcohol and their violation of the fundamentalist view of strict observance of the sabbath. Many members of the laboring classes resented them because some immigrants were often willing to work for lower wages than the prevailing ones. Protestants were hostile because many of the immigrants were Irish and German Catholics, whom they feared as possible subverters of the public schools and of the republican form of government.

Politicians made capital out of the fears and apprehensions of numerous insecure citizens by transforming the anti-immigration movement into a political crusade that found expression in the American Nativist, or Know-Nothing, party. By the time of the Civil War, the dream of a pluralistic society seemed to be more of a nightmare than a modus vivendi for an increasingly complex social organism.

In the years following the Civil War, the United States matured in a number of ways. The industrial growth that had been so greatly stimulated by the war now became one of the wonders of the world. The population of the country increased at a staggering rate, from thirty-nine million in 1870 to more than one hundred million at the time of the nation's entry into World War I. The flow of migrants from the countries of northern and western Europe was greatly augmented by the millions that came from southern and eastern Europe and from Japan and China. In 1865 one white American authority, Dr. C. K. Marshall, had confidently predicted that the Afro-American population would disappear altogether by January 1, 1920; but that group had increased from a healthy four and one-half million in 1870 to a thumping nine million by the time of Dr. Marshall's "day of judgment" in 1920. Meanwhile, the population shift from rural to urban areas was at least as dramatic as the population increase itself. And with the extensive urbanization of the United States in the last quarter of the nineteenth century, the problems attending the concentration of the population in urban centers were magnified several times over.

Surely, one of the most complex and, indeed, one of the most urgent problems was how could so many millions of people of such diverse racial, religious, cultural, and national backgrounds live in peace, in mutual respect, and contribute to the well-being of each other and of the nation. It was not an easy task on the face of it. It was made much more difficult by several factors. First, there was the agitation for immigration restriction that would prevent the coming of the families of those already arrived and whose exclusion constituted a repudiation of the principle of an open society of which the nation boasted. Second, there was the growing respectability and influence of the principles of Social Darwinism that gave sanction to the ruthless oppression of disadvantaged persons in the name of the "survival of the fittest." Last, there was the blatant and unmitigated racial and religious bigotry that was tolerated more than the egalitarian principles on which the nation claimed to be founded.

Perhaps the anniversary of the nation's Centennial would provide an opportunity for the people to give some attention to this problem. It was an auspicious year. At the great exhibition in Philadelphia, the miracle of the telephone was placed on public display for the first time; and it could be said, as Henry Adams was to say of the Paris Exposition of 1900, that the visitors could view the enormous machinery and the powerful motors as a moral force, "much as the early Christians felt the Cross." But it would take maturity, a sense of purpose, and even wisdom to define and then pursue the two goals of national fulfillment and individual and group integrity.

From such high purposes there were distractions enough. It was the Centennial year, but it was also the worst year of the nation's worst depression; and many wondered if the economy would ever bottom out. It was the year of a presidential election, one of the most bitterly fought for many a decade; and when the contest ended in dispute, there were those who despaired of the survival of the Union. Even so, the high purposes were not altogether ignored. Almost everywhere, there was a quickening of the national consciousness as southerners and northerners alike celebrated the centennial of independence. Throughout the land there was a strong movement to place higher education within the reach of everyone; and in the decade of the 1870s alone some 112 colleges and universities were founded. Their very diversity bespeaks the remarkably broad spectrum of interests—both black and white, in the context of the nineteenth century— to be served by their establishment. There were women's colleges such as Bennett, Wellesley, Smith, and Radcliffe; sectarian institutions such as Hebrew Union College, Calvin College, and Loyola University of Chicago; nonsectarian institutions such as Johns Hopkins University, Meharry Medical College, and the George Peabody College for Teachers; and public institutions such as the universities of Colorado and Oregon and Prairie View State and Hunter colleges.

The professionalization of the nation's educational and cultural leadership that was promoted by the growth of institutions of higher education provided some assurance that these institutions would not fall prey to the political opportunists who had little or no interest in the life of the mind. The teachers colleges, the educational associations, and the professional magazines raised the consciousness and self-respect of teachers and librarians alike who began to appreciate even more than in the past their responsibilities as guardians of the nation's heritage. In this connection two significant developments occurred in the centennial year of the nation's independence. One was, of course, the founding of the American Library Association in Philadelphia a few months after the independence Centennial celebration. At a time when other areas of intellectual activity were making a self-conscious attempt to define their roles in American society, librarians undertook to define what they were doing in quite professional terms, to establish standards for service in the profession, and to spell out their role in the cultural and educational life of the nation. The other development was the establishment of the *Library Journal,* which proved to be a most important instrument for the improvement and promotion of modern librarianship.

With the exception of two vast umbrella organizations, the National Education Association and the American Association for the Advancement of Science that had been founded before the Civil War, no other professional societies had been founded in the United States by 1876. (Such learned societies as the American Philosophical Society and the American Antiquarian Society had, of course, been in existence for a long time.) In that year the American Library Association was to share pioneering honors with the American Chemical Society; the historians, economists, and others did not formally organize until 1884 and later. In the make-up of its own membership, the American Library Association had a certain heterogeneity that suggested the pluralism of American society, not so much in racial and national terms as in the diversity of the professional and personal interests of its members. The membership represented virtually all types of libraries—private, public, society, law, medical, theological. There were men and women, laymen and professionals, "conservatives and liberals, visionaries and standpatters." They were bound together as, indeed, the nation was bound together, by a strong commitment to a common enterprise that transcended philosophical and professional differences and placed worthy common objectives over other less important considerations.

This was by no means an easy task; but it was not impossible. First, they had to adopt some form of science in their work, as John W. Wallace, the president of the Historical Society of Pennsylvania, suggested in his address of welcome. They should do this "lest they be buried in the very mass of books they were handling." With talented and resourceful leaders such as Melvil Dewey and Charles A. Cutter in the forefront, the science of librarianship was assured. Second, they had to promote the profession among would-be practitioners; and through the *Library Journal,* the committee on library training of the American Library Association, and such pioneer institutions as the Columbia School of Library Economy, it was possible for members of the profession to set and maintain high standards of performance. Third, the general public—not merely the highly educated public—had to be made aware of the importance of the library as a cultural and educational institution. In a variety of ways the local and national organizations of librarians could and did educate the public, while, at the same time, bringing pressure to bear on government at every level to provide adequate support for their institutions. As Dewey said, "we are forced to divide popular education into two parts of almost equal importance and deserving equal attention: the free school and the free library." Finally, the librarians had to join forces with other elements in the population to make certain that libraries and all other cultural and educational institutions were established and maintained in the service of all segments of the population.

Once the profession of librarianship had become well established and once the libraries themselves were recognized as important to the culture and education of the people, the librarians would still have to face real problems and assume clear responsibilities in their professional roles. One of these was the need to recognize the all important principle that the true diffusion of knowledge rejects discriminatory practices or practices of exclusion against certain groups and individuals because of race, religion, political or social views, or national origin. Apparently not even Melvil Dewey was free from certain biases that could have affected his practices as a librarian. While director of the State Library of New York, the enterprising Dewey was also managing the Lake Placid Club, which excluded from membership all Jews "even when of unusual personal qualifications." He argued that it was not his personal bias but a regulation of the club that excluded them. The regents rejected this explanation when they discovered that Dewey and his wife owned a majority of the stock in the Lake Placid Company, "which in turn owned and managed the Club's property." With all his reforming zeal and with all of his progressive ideas, it seems clear that Dewey had prejudices against at least one group. One wonders how much of this was reflected in his administration of the State Library of New York. This weakness in a person of Dewey's strength is a dramatic reminder that librarians and, indeed, all others who presume to guard and promote the nation's culture and education betray their trust when they countenance the exclusion of any group from the enjoyment of the opportunity to utilize a community's cultural and educational facilities.

Another responsibility of librarians was to steer clear of those extra-professional forces that sought to subvert the principles of a free and open society. These outside influences could be quite powerful. In the field of public education, for example, George Peabody had said in the 1870s that he would withdraw his generous support from schools in the South if the Civil Rights Act required white and black children to attend the same schools. Consequently, members of Congress dutifully deleted from the act the provision calling for the desegregation of the schools. This postponed any serious consideration of the matter for almost one hundred years. In the library field the influence could be seen in the role of Andrew Carnegie, whose philanthropy led to the establishment of scores of libraries in the United States and abroad. In some instances, as in Pittsburgh, Carnegie insisted on naming a majority of the members of the library board, presumably to keep the institution out of politics. In other instances, as in each southern community where he set up a library, Carnegie permitted local whites to control the situation. This meant that some communities allocated all of the Carnegie money to the library for whites, without any provision at all for a library for Negroes. Meanwhile some other communities allocated most of the Carnegie money for the library for whites, assigning the remainder to a hopelessly inferior library for blacks. One searches in vain for an indignant outcry on the part of the professional librarians against this profanation of their sacred profession and this subversion of their cherished institutions. Libraries could scarcely function effectively in a pluralistic society if they adhered to principles that denied a healthy respect for the several groups that made up that society.

In this same vein, librarians would need to oppose the distribution of public funds that called for the generous support of libraries for, say, whites while providing for a quite inadequate support of libraries for blacks. Many state library commissions, county boards, and city councils in many parts of the country were as callous and indifferent in the support of Negro libraries as they were in their support of Negro schools. As recently as 1935, as Eliza Gleason has shown, the amounts spent for Negro library service bore little relation to such factors as wealth of the community and the proportion of the black population. Indeed, until the recent cases involving public education and the passage of the Civil Rights Act of 1964, public libraries for blacks in the South and in the ghettoes of the North were not serving in a manner to promote the healthy growth of a pluralistic society.

If, through their policies, libraries and librarians have, at times, reflected the darker phases of American society, it can be said that they have, on occasion, risen to a higher level and reflected the better aspects of the American ideal to which one can point with pride. To a considerable extent they have been responsible for raising our level of appreciation for the heritage of the various cultures that make up American society. If historians and others have celebrated American pluralism in their writings, libraries and librarians have been the major purveyors and promoters of these writings. If various ethnic, racial, and national groups have underscored the contributions of their respective heritages, the libraries, perhaps more than any other institution, have called them to the attention of the American public. If the patriots have made much of the complexity and diversity of this country, the libraries have translated these qualities into popular consciousness and understanding. If these complexities and diversities have, at times, led to misunderstanding and conflict, the libraries, by emphasizing the positive aspects, have done much to resolve the conflicts and restore mutual respect and confidence among the combatants.

It has been the library, moreover, that has facilitated the remarkable explosion of knowledge over the past century. Secure in what Wallace in 1876 called the "science of their work," librarians have been in a position not only to serve scholarship but also to make an imaginative and constructive contribution to scholarship as well. One shudders to contemplate the fate of the American scholar without the intimate association and partnership with the American librarian. How rash and imprudent would be any scholar to suggest that he could have achieved even a fraction of what he achieved without the advice and understanding of the reference librarian, the serials librarian, the microfilm librarian, the interlibrary loan librarian, the subject field librarian, the manuscripts librarian, and a well-stocked collection of books, periodicals, and other materials as well. If there are those among us who immodestly boast that they have pushed back the frontiers of learning or have made discoveries that have contributed to knowledge, those same persons must humbly concede that such knowledge would be of little use without the libraries and their personnel who are the principal organizers of the new knowledge as well as the old.

As librarians observe the Centennial of the American Library Association, they have many reasons to be pleased with their contributions to the life of the mind in the United States. They know, better than one could recount here, just what these contributions have been. Without them and the institutions they serve, this country would be a veritable intellectual and cultural desert thoroughly incapable of coping with its own major problems in that area. The Americans are very few indeed who would be content to deal with such problems without the assistance and support of one of the nation's most important cultural resources. Those who would feel that they are better off without such assets are even fewer, if they exist at all.

One cannot ever rest on one's laurels however great they may be and however tempting that posture of repose may be. And, indeed, the laurels of American librarianship are more a challenge than a benediction. For the profession has been so much a part of this nation's ambivalence and inconsistency regarding the objective and impartial diffusion of knowledge in a pluralistic society as to suggest that it has much to do yet to prove its intellectual independence and leadership.

If our libraries are to function effectively in a pluralistic society and if they are to provide today the kind of ingenious leadership that Dewey, Cutter, Poole, Winsor, and others provided a century ago, they must address themselves to today's problems in a creative, forthright manner. They must recognize the concept of pluralism not as an excuse for explaining away a certain group's religious, racial, or cultural idiosyncrasies but as an indication of the group's integrity that renders it even more worthy of participating in the total social order and contributing its special talents and experiences to the whole. In this context the library becomes the vehicle not for the continued cultural and intellectual isolation of Chicanos but the means by which others can come to understand the rich and ancient heritage of that group. In this context the people of Appalachia can view the library as a means by which they can overcome the isolation that has entrapped them for centuries and enter the larger stage of American life and culture. In this context libraries can expiate their guilt for the role that they have played in the degradation of blacks for a century by celebrating their role in building the nation's rich heritage for three centuries, not merely as Africans but as Americans in the way that Europeans became Americans.

A pluralistic society is not a collection of disparate groups whose differences are emphasized in order to justify and rationalize artificial separations and distinctions, as has often been the case. Rather, a pluralistic society is a collection of peoples rich in their diverse heritages whose contributions to the whole make them worthy participants in the building of a richer and better social order. Libraries in such a setting can be a principal instrument in weaving a tapestry of pluralism and in communicating its beauty and richness to the several strands that make it up. In the years ahead, libraries, with their personnel so adept in the "science of their work," can do much to create a social order of peace, purposefulness, and mutual respect such as we have never known before.

Dan Mabry Lacy

Senior Vice-President, McGraw-Hill, Inc.

Mr. Lacy is a member of the National Commission on New Technological Uses of Copyrighted Works (CONTU) appointed by the President of the United States in 1975. After joining the National Archives staff in 1942, he became Assistant Archivist in 1947. Later that year, Mr. Lacy went to the Library of Congress as Assistant Director of the Processing Department. He was appointed Deputy Chief Assistant Librarian in 1950. From 1951 to 1953 he was in the State Department as Assistant Administrator of the International Information Agency, in charge of the USIS book and library program. For his work there, he was awarded the Department's Superior Service Medal in 1952. He left government service in 1953 to become Managing Director of the American Book Publisher's Council. He joined McGraw-Hill as Senior Vice-President in 1966. He is noted for his efforts to bring closer liaison between the library and publishing professions and for his contributions to intellectual freedom. His books include *Freedom and Communication* (1961).

LIBRARIES AND THE FREEDOM OF ACCESS
TO INFORMATION

I TAKE MY TEXT from two distinguished Virginians. One is William
Berkeley, who served as the able and domineering governor of the colony
during two long stretches of the seventeenth century. The other is James
Madison, principal architect of the Constitution and the Bill of Rights and
later President of the United States.

> Said Berkeley: "I thank God, there are no free schools nor printing,
> and I hope we shall not have these hundred years; for learning has
> brought disobedience, and heresy, and sects into the world, and
> printing has divulged them, and libels against the best govern-
> ment. God keep us from both."
> Said Madison: "A popular Government, without popular informa-
> tion, or the means of acquiring it, is but a Prologue to a Farce or a
> Tragedy; or perhaps both. Knowledge will forever govern igno-
> rance: And a people who mean to be their own Governors, must
> arm themselves with the power which knowledge gives."[1]

These two men, so different in all else, agreed on one thing: knowledge
is power. Access to knowledge is access to power. A society that believes
that power should belong to the chosen few will restrict knowledge, or at
least important knowledge, to that few. But one that believes that power
belongs to the people will open knowledge to the people too. And one that
believes in equality will open it equally.

However imperfectly it has adhered to it over the years, our society from
the beginning committed itself to the principle that power belongs to the
people, and to them individually and equally. The philosophers of the

19

Revolution recognized that this daring idea demanded for its success that if power were to be widely distributed, so too must knowledge be.

George Washington, John Adams, Thomas Jefferson, Benjamin Rush, and a host of others shared the conviction that the Republic could survive and prosper only if the people generally, who now shared power, shared knowledge as well. "And say, finally," asked Jefferson in a letter to Madison in 1787, "whether peace is best preserved by giving energy to the government, or information to the people. This last is the most certain, and the most legitimate engine of government. Educate and inform the whole mass of the people. Enable them to see that it is their interest to preserve peace and order, and they will preserve them."

What I want to do here is to give some thought to the public policies the United States has adopted to achieve that general and equal access to knowledge which our forefathers saw as prerequisite to equal political and economic opportunity and to free government itself and to consider the role of libraries within that broader context.

Time does not permit any detailed attention to the history of those policies; but we may note certain highlights in passing. The Founding Fathers proved unwilling, with rare exceptions, to devote public funds to schools or libraries or other means of conveying knowledge. They were content to leave this to private efforts; but in the very dawn of the Republic, they did adopt two fundamental measures to protect and encourage those private efforts. One was the first federal copyright act which established a legal framework for authorship and publishing. The other was the First Amendment, which protected the freedom of writers and speakers and of the churchmen whose pulpits and schools were themselves important instruments of communication.

Leaving education in private hands meant leaving it to the well-to-do, but an education was not yet the key to opportunity it later became. A man did not need letters to carve a farm from the wilderness, and a scant-schooled Washington could found a nation. As the century passed, however, and the commercial economy burgeoned, reading, writing, and arithmetic became a price of success. And Jacksonian egalitarianism demanded that the opportunities literacy brought be open to all—or at least to all white men. The tax-supported common school was society's response. By the Civil War it was found almost everywhere in the North and was taking widespread root in the South.

While public policy was opening opportunity to most white men, it all but ignored white women and closed every door to blacks. No schools were open to blacks in the South and only the poorest segregated schools were available in the North. To teach a Negro to read was a crime in the South, and North and South alike used censorship, closure of the mails, beatings, burnings, and murder to stop the issuance of publications that would inform blacks of their human rights or encourage them to seek those rights.

The modern revolution in access to information, however, came in the last quarter of the nineteenth century. We became a nation of cities and factories, bound together by a network of rails. The whole urban labor force had to be literate. Vast numbers required higher training in science and technology and the professions to manage the explosively grown new economy. A steady flood of technical, market, and financial information was needed to keep it going.

The response, both public and private, was massive. Universal elementary education, at least for whites, became not only an ideal but also a fact. Millions of immigrants were ground through the Americanization process of urban school systems. Land grant colleges with open enrollment and low tuition were established to give all who sought it the practical training in scientific agriculture, engineering, and technology the new economy required. Mechanical and chemical processes for making cheap paper from wood pulp, high-speed, steam-powered, rotary presses, and a highly organized publishing industry poured out a mass literature in books, magazines, and newspapers to match the mass literacy the schools were creating. By a singularly far-sighted piece of legislation, Congress in 1879 established the second-class postal rate, permitting magazines and newspapers to use the new rail system to reach into every county of the nation with a low, uniform postal rate. It gave us for the first time a national press.

The modern public library movement and this Association both had their birth in this era. For the first time, print became potentially open to all.

But while this was happening, society decided to continue the exclusion of blacks and Indians from equal participation in its government and its benefits. After a first flurry of effort during Reconstruction, the North abandoned the education of blacks to southern whites, who were determined that blacks in legal freedom as in slavery should continue in their role as an agricultural and domestic labor force, supported only at the margin of subsistence and barred from political influence or educational opportunity. This end was achieved by closing white schools, white colleges, and white libraries to blacks and allowing only the barest minimum of education in segregated schools. Any training above the primary grades was forced into the pattern of vocational education, and that only in farming and domestic service. To withhold knowledge was once more to withhold power.

With the closing of the frontier, the Indians, whose lands had been steadily encroached upon, were segregated and moved to reservations. Here, too, only feeble efforts at education were made, and the Native Americans remained outside the liberating flow of knowledge as they remained outside the other mainstreams of the alien life around them.

Over the first four decades of the twentieth century, the information system created in the late nineteenth century matured and expanded, but changed little in its fundamentals. Elementary schools improved greatly in quality, especially in rural areas as the automobile and the school bus made possible larger consolidated schools. The high school became as universally available as the elementary school, though only about half the youth of the country troubled to win its diplomas. Radio and newsreel added major new instruments for spreading news, and film offered an important, if rarely effectively used, means of enriching education. Libraries were vastly enlarged and improved.

But print remained the basic means of communication. A college education or any form of professional training remained an exception, available to perhaps one youth in a dozen. Most Indians remained cut off from any really effective participation in the national information system. In the southern and border states where most blacks still lived, they were still barred from white schools, white colleges, and white libraries, and the segregated institutions available to them were far inferior even to the not very strong schools, colleges, and libraries available to southern whites.

There were marked regional and class, as well as racial, inequities in the availability of knowledge. Louis Round Wilson in his studies of the geography of reading called attention to the dramatic differences in library service available in the southern states and in the rest of the country. An equally dramatic contrast could have been drawn between the excellent service provided by the great urban public libraries, the meager service (if any) available in small towns, and the almost wholly nonexistent service to rural areas. Within large cities, branch libraries in black areas almost always had weaker collections and poorer services than those in white. The levels of school and college support followed the same geographic patterns.

Everywhere the well-to-do had a more abundant access to better schools and larger libraries than were available to the poor. At one extreme were the great private universities, barring almost all blacks and able to be very selective among whites, drawing their students largely from the great eastern preparatory schools and from the children of alumni. At the other were the one-room rural schools that were the end of education for many farm children throughout the country, the absence of schooling beyond the most meager beginnings for millions of Indian, black, and Oriental Americans, the long stretches of rural area with no library service, the tens of millions of Americans who remained illiterate measured by any functional test. From the first-rate schools, the great universities, the library-served cities came most of those who made up the American establishment—the leaders of professions, the masters of industries, the counselors to rulers. In the other environment lived the poor. Those who were cut off from full access to knowledge were cut off as well from power and prosperity. Ignorance, poverty, and powerlessness bred each other in an endless cycle.

In part this isolation and subordination of the poor and nonwhite were due to the lack of means to do better. But in part it was deliberate choice of those with power. The existence of a large mass of men and women with little or no education meant that there was available a large force for unskilled labor on farms or in sweat shops who lacked both bargaining power for higher wages and the knowledge that would enable them to organize to assert their rights or obtain political power. In the South, compulsory education was often opposed for white children as well as black on the explicit and openly stated grounds that the country needed few leaders and managers but large numbers of workers for their hard, poorly paid, but necessary labor—workers not stirred into discontent by education.

An even greater revolution in the access to knowledge than that of the late nineteenth century came in the years following World War II. The war itself contributed a powerful surge. Fought against the most evil and racist of tyrannies, it forced a reevaluation of our own ideals of equality and some recognition of our own racism. The bringing together of millions of young Americans in the armed forces on a more or less egalitarian though still almost entirely segregated basis reinforced this conviction. And it also revealed the unsuspected proportions and the crippling effect of illiteracy and ignorance.

On the positive side, the enormous contribution of science and advanced technology to the winning of the war, culminating in the invention of the atomic bomb, gave knowledge a new and awesome prestige in our society.

The most significant of our early responses to this new perception of the power of knowledge and the goal of equality was the enactment of the G.I. Bill of Rights. There had been some provision, in pensions or public lands, for the veterans of all past wars. But now all veterans were offered a college education at public expense. It was a revolutionary concept. In pre-World War II America the college degree had increasingly become the symbol of privilege and position—socially, politically, and economically— the demarcation line between the executive and professional on one side, the foremen and workers on the other. In pre-Civil War America a man with very limited education, like Washington, Jackson, and Lincoln, could become President and be among our greatest; but in the century following Andrew Johnson, Harry Truman was the only President not a college man. In an earlier day, the Wright brothers, Edison, Ford, and Rockefeller could be towering figures in invention and in business without college training; but by the 1920s and 1930s a man without a degree had no more chance to become president of a major corporation than he did to be President of the United States. In the wartime army the degree has been the usual boundary between officer and enlisted man.

Now this door to standing and success was to be opened to all. Any man with brains and energy enough could become a college graduate and join the elite. From that time forward, the majority of young men carried their education beyond high school. Though few women benefited from the G.I. Bill, the perception of a college education as the normal rather than the rare and exceptional experience of young Americans extended to women as well. And it persisted long after the exhaustion of their educational benefits by the World War II veterans. In the decades since 1945, more than half of all young Americans continued their education beyond high school, and a very high proportion completed college degrees. By the hundreds of thousands they went on for postgraduate and professional education. Expanded by population growth as well, the number of young people in college in 1970 was nearly 10 times as great as in the pre-war years.

The second revolutionary step was begun with the decision of the United States Supreme Court that held in the Brown case that racially segregated school systems were unconstitutional. The immediate results in improving the access of blacks to adequate education was small. The southern states by massive resistance to the Court's decision avoided its effective implementation for years. The school systems of northern cities were already nominally integrated and hence unaffected. Border schools were promptly desegregated, but population moves, primarily of whites to suburbs, quickly restored de facto segregation. But a commitment to black equality was set in the law and could not be easily escaped.

An acute awareness of the need for major investment in library resources to meet post-war social and educational needs was rapidly growing in the 1950s. The great increase in efforts devoted to research and development and the consequent outpouring of books, journals, and research reports created an urgent demand for enlarged research libraries and, in particular, for the development of advanced data storage and retrieval and bibliographical systems. Colleges and universities were expanding overnight and upgrading their offerings. Hundreds of institutions were being transformed from colleges into universities or founded anew. The tidal wave of post-war students was pressing its way into elementary school. In suburban counties and in such states as California and Florida elementary school enrollments were quadrupling, with new schools that needed libraries springing up overnight. Deficiencies in the quality of education were being increasingly noted. Rural areas, having recovered from deep economic depression as a result of the wartime demand for farm products, were insisting on better schools and library service. The creation of the National Book Committee and the National Library Week helped to mobilize opinion leaders behind the demands for better library support.

State and local funding for education and libraries increased dramatically in the 1950s and 1960s, and by the late 1950s federal funds began slowly to be appropriated. The Library Services Act of 1956 was the first federal support for other than federal libraries. It authorized funds for the expansion of library service to previously unserved rural areas. In 1958 the National Defense Education Act provided funding for school libraries to acquire books, other than textbooks, relating to science, mathematics and modern foreign languages, and also audiovisual materials.

The really revolutionary application of federal funds to information availability came, however, in the mid-1960s. Improvements in agricultural technology—cotton-picking machines, chemical herbicides, and shifts to less labor-intensive land uses—had displaced millions of blacks, poor whites, Puerto Ricans, and Mexican peasants, who had moved in enormous numbers to the larger cities of the upper Midwest, the Northeast, and the Pacific Coast.

In the new urban environment their serious educational deprivation, so long unnoticed on remote farms, became painfully evident. Marginal literacy at best and ignorance of modern industrial and clerical work left many of them essentially unemployable. With the social structures of church and work groups and of neighborhoods destroyed by the migration, they became a rootless and anarchic group in the cities, beset by unemployment, poverty, alcoholism, drug addiction, and crime. Welfare, medical, and police costs to the cities rose frighteningly.

For generations white society had undertaken to exclude blacks from any access to economic opportunity or political power by denying or stifling access to knowledge. Now it was reaping the fruit of that exclusion.

A frightened concern for welfare costs and crime in the streets paired with shocked social consciences produced a determination to break through the circle of poverty and ignorance, each engendering the other. A "war on poverty" was declared. Just as exclusion from educational opportunity and sources of knowledge had been one of the principal instruments for holding blacks and poor whites in economic and political subordination, so improved education and access to information were now to be the means of integrating those groups more productively into the economy.

There were several weapons in the war on poverty. One was the Elementary and Secondary Education Act of 1965, which for the first time committed major federal funds to education and provided that most of the more than a billion and a half dollars initially authorized should go to local schools in proportion to the number of the children enrolled who came from poverty-stricken homes. This meant that the funds went largely to the core city schools of great metropolitan areas and to southern rural school systems. A substantial sum was committed to school libraries, and in the early years of the program this was supplemented by the use of a large part of the general funds under the act for school library support. As a result, many urban school systems, like that of New York City, got their first elementary school libraries. For the first time, too, schools and libraries devoted primarily to children of poor urban racial minorities had money to enter the marketplace and demand books suited to their users. In consequence there was a serious effort to publish children's books with black or Chicano or Puerto Rican characters and environments.

The Head Start program was initiated to give disadvantaged children a better preparation for school. Under the Economic Opportunity Act, Job Corps and similar programs gave an opportunity for training and productive entry into the economy for those who had left school.

A major drive was opening colleges, universities, and professional schools to blacks and members of other minority groups. Changing admission standards and tutoring and other special assistance programs helped undo the discrimination that was the by-product of early denials of educational opportunity to blacks. Black college enrollment increased sharply. The Supreme Court's anti-segregation decision began to be seriously enforced.

On a much smaller scale, there were similar efforts to improve Indian educational opportunity and library and other information services, though with limited success.

Public libraries, whose users have come principally from well-educated members of the middle class, also made efforts to redirect their services toward the needs of disadvantaged, largely black and Hispanic, members of their communities. The federal Library Services Act (now Services and Construction) had been broadened to include urban as well as rural libraries, and it provided much of the funding for "outreach" programs designed to bring the library's services to those who had not been among its traditional users.

Other federal aid was granted to college libraries and, through the programs of the Library of Congress and the National Library of Medicine, to centralized bibliographical service.

In 1966 President Johnson appointed a National Advisory Commission on Libraries to prepare recommendations for a unified national policy on library services. Its report, submitted to President Johnson in July 1968, presented as its fundamental recommendation "That it be declared National Policy, enunciated by the President and enacted into law by the Congress, that the American people should be provided with library and informational services adequate to their needs, and that the Federal Government, in collaboration with state and local governments and private agencies, should exercise leadership in assuring the provision of such needs."

By legislation by the following Congress, this was indeed declared to be the national policy of the United States and a permanent Commission on Libraries and Information Science was established to plan and report on its execution.

The private sector of the society responded even more dramatically than the public to the post-war generation's need for vastly more information and for more widely and equally distributed information.

Part of this response was simply quantitative; the total number of books published per year grew from 7,500 in 1947 to 41,000 in 1974, and the number of magazines and journals more than doubled. Much of this increase was in direct response to public programs. Most of the increase in magazines and journals, for example, occurred in the number of scholarly and scientific journals responding to the great increase in federal expenditure in support of research. The increase in the number of books published also included a doubling or tripling of advanced works in scholarly fields. There was an even larger increase in the number of children's books, directly responding to the multiplication of school libraries. In content as well, they reflected public programs, with a greater attention to the needs and interests of children of racial minorities.

But the really dramatic developments in the private sector involved new products or technological achievements. There were three of special importance.

One was the coming of the modern paperback book, which had its beginnings just before World War II but achieved its role only in the decade after the war. Paperbacks increased by at least fivefold the number of books bought by individuals for their own reading. Because they were cheap and available at outlets everywhere, paperbacks were a powerful force for the democratization of reading. Especially has this become the case since paperback publishing has expanded from a limited number of romances, mysteries, and westerns to the point at which more than 100,000 paperbacks are in print, embracing substantially the entire body of standard literature.

The second was the coming of television, probably the most important development in communication since printing. More than 97 percent of American homes now have television, and the average American spends hundreds of hours a year watching it. It is by far the most egalitarian of the information media. Perhaps one American in fifty buys a hardcover book at least once a year; perhaps one in thirty belongs to a book club; one in six buys paperbacks; one in four uses a public library. Substantially all watch television. There is a vast difference in what different kinds of people draw from print—indeed one of the glories of print is its infinite adaptability to individual interests and needs. The physicist, the historian, the business man, the vacation reader, the inner city youth—all draw very different things from books, magazines, and newspapers. Abler, better educated, and more powerful men and women can use print effectively to gain skills and information they need to increase their power. Handicapped by difficulty in reading, lack of knowledge of sources, and the relative unavailability of materials, poor and ignorant men and women have little success in using print for their purposes.

There are, of course, different levels of television usages as well. One man may watch public affairs discussions or serious drama on educational TV while another watches bowling or westerns. But essentially the flow of information about current events, about Watergate and Viet Nam and the economy, is the same for all. There are dangers in this to which I shall allude later. But the most important fact is that for the first time in our history those who cannot or do not make effective use of print can still be informed about the world around them at much the same level as more privileged citizens. This has had a profound effect on the power and effectiveness of minority groups. Blacks, Chicanos, students, women, and others who have felt themselves treated unfairly by society have had an opportunity to see their issues defined, to observe the protests of others, and to achieve a unity of conviction. Though network television has been accused both of banality and of imposing uniformity of thought, for most Americans it has been a large and stimulating addition to the knowledge and ideas at their command. And to smaller communities across the country, set in traditional and conventional views, the effect of network TV is not to impose uniformity but to introduce a healthy diversity on such issues as racial or social equality.

A more recent development, of major potential importance, is cable TV, multiplying the number of possible channels and making it practical for viewers to pay for the programming they want.

The third development is the electronic computer, playing an even larger part in our lives. Early conceptions that computer memories would be the repository of complete texts, replacing printed media, have diminished, with a better understanding of the computer's potential. But its capacity to record, manipulate, select, and call up individual data has become more powerful and less expensive. Enormous power is created by the existence of information system based on data banks. At present, this power resides primarily in large corporations and in government agencies that can make the very large investment in equipment and programming required. But it makes possible the efficient administration of exceedingly complex undertakings of both administration and research; it has enormous power as a bibliographical tool; and it makes it possible to consolidate and maintain records on individuals with alarming efficiency.

This wealth of information resources and means of dissemination now available to us, and the clear commitments of national policy in the late 1960s, seemed to open the way to a more abundant and a more equal dissemination of information than any nation had ever had. But even before the end of the Johnson Administration there was a turning away from this goal as the tragedy of Viet Nam blighted the promising surge of his Great Society programs. And in the Nixon Administration there was a dramatic reversal of policy. Cuts were sought in all programs of aid to education. The Nixon budgets sought to delete every penny of federal funding for nonfederal libraries—public, school, and college. The newly created National Commission on Libraries and Information Science was inadequately funded and given little or no attention. Programs like Head Start and the Job Corps, aimed at improving the educational opportunities of disadvantaged children and youths, were eliminated or sharply reduced. Other decisions or policies aimed at giving the poor information needed for their protection were attacked, such as the Miranda decision requiring that those arrested be told of their rights, and programs for legal assistance to the poor in their dealings with public authority. There was an almost paranoid effort to avoid leaks of information from government sources, including a novel and sweeping claim of executive privilege that would have allowed the President, at his sole discretion, to conceal any information about acts of the government even from Congress and the courts. Menacing pressure was brought to bear on the press and especially on television to avoid criticism of the Administration, and book publishers were confronted with suits imposing prior restraints on the publication of information the government wished to suppress.

One hopes that that nightmare is now behind us and that we can return to the reconstruction of a national policy on access to information and to the role of libraries in such a policy. We need to remember that libraries are but one component in a total national system of communication embracing schools, colleges, universities, books, magazines, newspapers, films, radio, and television. Indeed, libraries are a very small component in that total system if one were to measure their role by comparing the man-hours spent annually in using library materials with the man-hours spent annually in reading printed material from other sources—books, magazines, newspapers, trade journals, pamphlets, etc.—in listening to radio, and in watching films and TV. Of the total flow of information to the American people, the proportion that comes through the library is a tiny one.

But if the role of libraries is small, it is crucial. All the other media of our society increase the power of the single speaker or writer, linking him or her to ever vaster audiences, reaching their peak in prime-time network television, when a President may reach fifty million or more at one moment. Alone among the instruments of communication, the library throws its weight on the opposite side of the scale, increasing the power of the single inquirer by linking him or her with an ever vaster number of sources of information. The library brings that leaven of individual choice, that opening of power to the single stubborn and inquiring mind, that leavens and uplifts the whole mass of our enormous communications system, repairing and healing its other deficiencies.

There are many aspects of a sensible national policy on access to information that do not directly involve libraries. They involve especially education in all its aspects and television, including cable and pay television and public television. Many other federal programs and regulations, like postal rates, materially affect access to information. Perhaps most important of all is the policy of the federal government with regard to access to information about its own activities and to that contained in its own data bases. For the government generates incomparably more data about the American people and the environment they live in than any other source; it finances most of the research in medicine, nuclear physics, and many other areas of science; it underwrites curriculum development and the creation of new teaching materials in many areas of science and the humanities. Above all, it is the ultimate and often the sole source of knowledge on issues of the most crucial importance to us, in such areas as national defense, international relations, or nuclear energy.

I regret that time does not allow us to discuss the policy decisions that need to be made in these areas. Suffice it to say that we urgently need to reexamine all those policies against the test of how well they serve to open to all Americans the resources of knowledge. In all of them we need a resurrection of commitment.

But it is library policy that must here be the center of our concern. As recently as the report of the National Advisory Commission on Libraries in 1968 and the enactment of the statement on national policy on library service proposed in that report, the library community could see an expanding field of activity on every hand: federally supported development of major research collections, automated bibliographical and cataloging services, and the development of more sophisticated information systems would enable libraries to support swiftly expanding research efforts. Outreach programs, storefront libraries, library service for hospitals and prisons, bookmobiles in remote rural areas, and similar programs would bring library service to the unserved. County and multi-county systems would provide adequate central collections for service to smaller communities. Federal and state funding would enable libraries at all levels from primary grades to professional and postgraduate to play an even larger role in education. Through libraries access to information would be freed, enlarged, and enriched at every level of society.

Within a few short years this burgeoning program has collapsed, its golden hopes blasted. Great research institutions are reduced nearly to financial despair. Library services are among the first to be curtailed by hard-pressed educational institutions at every level from elementary school to post-graduate university. Urban library branches are closed, hours of service are curtailed, special reference services dropped, outreach programs abandoned. Library funds almost everywhere are declining in the face of rapid increases in the costs of personnel, materials, and utilities.

In this difficult time the library profession has looked to interlibrary cooperation and the creation of networks as the principal answer to its problems. Library literature is full of network proposals. They have achieved a measure of concrete realization in such organizations as OCLC and BALLOTS. The creation of a national library network is the principal thrust of the basic report of the National Commission on Libraries and Information Science. The argument for the necessity of such networks is often based on the argument that in view of the increase in the volume of material now being published, no library can any longer afford to acquire everything and to be self-sufficient.

The goals of most network proposals should obviously command our support. Certainly all must applaud the idea that libraries of the country, taken together, should be conceived as an integrated national resource. Centralization of cataloging and the making of bibliographic records to avoid wasteful duplication is an obvious necessity. Certainly, too, a planned division of labor is essential in collecting unusual and difficult to acquire materials of which only one or a few copies are needed nationally or in a region. Clearly federal support is needed for national and regional centers that undertake the systematic acquisition and cataloging of such material.

Especially do we need to improve the present hodge-podge, the controversial and inefficient system of obtaining copies of articles from journals not available in a user's own library. The present system requires searching to find a library willing to provide a copy, negotiation as to costs, delays in service, and a costly burden on the library providing the copy. It is usually without recompense to the journal publisher, who in the case of advanced scientific and scholarly journals relies almost totally on the library market for subscriptions. Availability of photocopies limits and may reduce his subscription list at a time of rapidly rising printing costs, threatening the extinction of some journals and skyrocketing subscription costs of others, further burdening the remaining subscribers. To the extent reliance must be placed on photocopies to provide service not otherwise realistically available, we earnestly need a system of recognized, efficient, publicly funded centers with adequate staff and collections licensed to provide photocopies and making through royalties or special subscription rates a pro rata contribution to the basic costs of producing the journal.[2]

And above all, it is an emphatically desirable, if as yet distant, national goal that everyone in the United States should have both bibliographical and actual access to whatever he or she needs from this total national resource.

Nevertheless, I am troubled by some of the arguments for networks—particularly the proposition that libraries cannot *any longer* be self-sufficient, as in the statement from a draft report of NCLIS that "Not even the largest library can any longer afford the cost of acquiring all the books and relevant information needed by their constituents." It's the "not any longer" that bothers me. Obviously no one ever had the notion that any library—not even the Bibliothèque Nationale or the British Museum or the Library of Congress—could acquire *everything* needed by their constituents or be self-sufficient. The "not any longer" obviously cannot really refer to self-sufficiency in any total sense. What then does it refer to? What is it that libraries formerly did that they cannot "any longer" afford to do?

I strongly suspect that what we really mean is that libraries can no longer afford to meet the normal day-to-day needs of their regular users. For a half century or more we have recognized that branch public libraries or college libraries, though perhaps fully adequate to meet the usual needs of their clients, would need to borrow on interlibrary loan materials required to meet unusual requests beyond their normal responsibilities. I suspect that networking now is being advanced on a very different basis. I suspect it is being advanced by hard-pressed library administrators and eagerly welcomed by harder pressed legislators and public officials not as a supplement to but as a substitute for adequate individual libraries.

We need to recognize the fact that dependence on central resources rather than on collections at hand, though obviously necessary for rarely called for materials not needed for regular service, is neither modern nor efficient, but slow, costly, and inefficient. Whenever we put forward networking or other forms of interlibrary cooperation in terms that allow it to be regarded as a *substitute* for, rather than an *addition* to, the adequate support of individual libraries, we do our cause, and the cause of access to information, great harm.

When a child goes to an elementary school that has no library, no com-

puter linkage with NELINET or SOLINET is going to meet his needs. Nor
is it going to meet the need of the high school dropout trying to find in the
public library branch something that can direct him to or prepare him for
job opportunities. It is not going to put a bookmobile into a farm community. It will not help the community college student whose young library
still lacks many of the basic reference materials for the courses he is taking.

Let us face the fact: In the library field the greatest limitation on access
to information in the United States is not at the level of access by the
specialist to complex data bases. It is simply the lack of adequately supported libraries. The basic problem is right there at the point of human
contact when the user finds or does not find the book or magazine or film
or information he needs. It can be solved very simply, if expensively, by
establishing and stocking adequate libraries adequately staffed with
trained librarians devoted to total community service. But there is no
other way, no cheap way, it can be solved.

A decade ago we were determined to provide those libraries and materials and services and were confident that we could. Perhaps that is what
the "not any longer" really refers to: that we no longer have that determination or confidence.

But it is nonsense to say we no longer can. We are a nation that could
afford to keep half a million men in Viet Nam year after year after year
and spend hundreds of billions of dollars on planes and bombs and mis-
siles to be used against that unfortunate country. We are the nation that
could afford to spend tens of billions of dollars to plant forever the foot-
prints of a few men in the moon's windless dust.

If we choose to do so, we can open access to the information every man,
woman, and child in the country needs—information that for most needs
will be at hand in the nearby library the user relies on. We can do it if
we will. Whether we will or not depends ultimately on what sort of society
we envision for America.

I return to what was said at the beginning, knowledge is power. It is
the key to participation in the service of our society and in its rewards. If
we believe that power belongs to the people generally, we will open knowledge to them generally. And if we believe in equality, we will open it

equally. If we believe in integrating excluded minorities into our whole society, we will find ways to extend the flow of information to embrace them. We are caught now in a time when social goals seem to have lost credibility and challenge, and when means do not seem to reach even to goals that have become weary and limited. But a better day will come when we emerge from our economic depression. The White House Conference on Libraries will give us a special chance to reconsider and restate our case. To be ready for the opportunities that will open, it is time we recaptured the fervor of our convictions of the 1950s and early 1960s and rededicated ourselves to those simple goals.

N O T E S

1. James Madison, quoted in Raoul Berger, *Executive Privilege: A Constitutional Myth* (Cambridge, Mass.: Harvard University Press, 1974), p. xv.

2. Since this address was delivered, the Copyright Act of 1976 has been passed. Its provisions on library photocopying do more to resolve conflicts in the present system than to lay the basis for a new and better system. But it provides for a review of those provisions in five years, and meanwhile the National Commission on New Technological Uses of Copyrighted Works (CONTU) is charged with further study of the problem. So is the National Commission on Libraries and Information Science (NCLIS). Their joint efforts should provide the information needed for a constructive solution. Authors, publishers, and librarians now seem jointly concerned about developing such a solution.

R. Kathleen Molz

Library journalist, administrator, and educator

From 1953 to 1956 Ms. Molz served on the staff of the Enoch Pratt Free Library in Baltimore. Appointed Television Specialist in 1957 at the Free Library of Philadelphia, she subsequently became its Public Relations Officer. From 1963 to 1968 she served as Editor of the *Wilson Library Bulletin*. Leaving for Washington in 1968, she became the Planning Officer for the federal library programs administered by the U.S. Office of Education, an experience she later described in her book *Federal Policy and Library Support*. At present she is Professor in the School of Library Service at Columbia University. Ms. Molz chaired the ALA Intellectual Freedom Committee from 1974 to 1975. She was elected to the Executive Board of ALA in 1976.

LIBRARIES AND THE DEVELOPMENT AND FUTURE
OF TAX SUPPORT

*W*HEN PRESIDENT HOLLEY wrote to me inviting me to give this address, he suggested that the topic "Libraries and the Development and Future of Tax Support" should be illuminated by an historical perspective and presented with some attention to present trends and future developments. Although I believe that I have followed this injunction, I have modified his request to place the topic within the context of paradox, for the issue of tax support for libraries in this country has been from the beginning fraught with contradictions and ambivalences both from those who sought it and those who made provision for it.

In a sense, I myself, quite innocently, am somewhat symptomatic of the bifurcated themes which I am about to describe to you. For I represent at least two traditions in the American Library Association, and I am not quite sure whether I was invited to typify either the one or the other or both. One of these relates to the choice of speaker; the other more precisely to the topic. Those of you who have followed closely the proceedings emanating from that first meeting of the Association called in 1876 will recall that even though Mr. [Lloyd] Smith encouraged the women delegates to speak up, the proceedings are singularly silent as to their comments. Buried, however, in a 1904 article in the *Library Journal,* entitled "Women in American Libraries," lies this overlooked bit of Associational history. The distinction of being the first woman to lift her voice in a meeting of the American Library Association belongs to the librarian of the Hartford (Connecticut) Public Library, Caroline M. Hewins, whose question posed in 1877 was "whether in any other state besides Massachusetts the income from the dog tax was used to support the public library."[1]

41

In a more serious vein, however, the second tradition relates quite closely to the topic of this address. Again, assiduous students of library history may remember that at that original ALA Conference the first librarian to speak after John William Wallace had given the address of welcome was William Frederick Poole, a giant of a man both in size and in accomplishment, who was then the librarian of the newly founded Chicago Public Library. The subject of Poole's address was "Some Popular Objections to Public Libraries," and he enumerated three, all of which were subsumed under the general heading of "that prolific source of political controversy," taxation. In what must truly remain the classic understatement of that initial convocation, Poole swept into his theme. "Libraries," he said, "cost money." And he added, "In every city and town of the land there is a feeling that the present rate of taxation is all that the property and business of the place will bear." In effect, then, the first objection to public libraries was "the universal dread of taxation"; the second, allied to the first, related to the inequity of the library tax, because some members of the public did not care to read while others preferred to pay for their books. In countering this second objection, Poole, after appropriately quoting from Mr. Jefferson, cited the "general welfare" provision of the U.S. Constitution, surely the first enunciation made by a librarian that the development of libraries lay within the purview of the national interest. The third objection is less easy to characterize, but stemmed from private conversations which Poole had had with those who complained that the new tax-supported libraries were a wasteful expenditure because they circulated novels and were generally indifferent to the concerns of scholarship. Rising to counter this third objection, Poole fulminated:

> In the public libraries which are growing up in our land, fully four-fifths of the money appropriated for books is spent in works adapted to the wants of scholars. In the larger libraries the proportion is even greater. It is hardly becoming for scholars, who enjoy the lion's share, to object to the small proportional expenditure for books adapted to the wants of the masses who bear the burden of taxation.[2]

One wonders if there were indeed criticisms of this sort, or if Poole merely summoned up straw men to make his point? Although it is abundantly clear to the modern-day reader that the main focus of Poole's speech was taxation, the index to that first volume of the *American Library Journal* in which it appears also provides for it the subject entry "Fiction, defended." That, too, must remain the verdict of that anonymous indexer concerning the contents of what must assuredly remain the historic address on the subject of library taxation.

Although Poole was solely concerned with public libraries, the intervening century has witnessed an array of the nation's librarians, pleading their cause before local, state, and federal officials. Today, revenues from the tax coffers of all three levels of government now support public, public school, governmental, and, in the case of those maintained as part of a state university or college, academic libraries. With the exception of special libraries in industrial plants or private businesses and of those with private endowment or in our private institutions of higher learning, almost every library in the nation is sustained wholly or in part by some form of public taxation. Yet, there is another substantive difference between the expression of Poole's concerns and our own, and that relates to the level of government occasioning the greatest interest. In 1876 Poole spoke only of the city and the town; today, at least from the amount of attention paid to it, the main focus of attention in the American Library Association seems to be the federal government. That fact, perhaps, is the first of the paradoxes since the economic role of the federal government in support of libraries is not particularly old nor has it ever been very sizable in total expenditures.

At this particular time, however, the federal government's position toward library support is highly ambiguous, and the gravity of the situation is no doubt heightened by the possibility that new federal legislation will soon be proposed by the National Commission on Libraries and Information Science, a program calling at least in part for the development of a nationwide network. Since the federal role seems to be most controversial and since the network has prompted so much discussion, both of these concepts figure prominently in this address. I shall begin—not with the inputs, that is, the taxes—but with the outputs, that is, the uses to which librarians have put tax monies.

From the time they first enjoyed professional identity, librarians in this country have entertained two significant goals, and for both they have sought governmental revenue. This, perhaps, is the second of the paradoxes, for these goals were sometimes so divergent that they might seemingly have been suggested by two different professions. The first relates to what we now call bibliographical control; the second, to the spread of literacy and the education of those whom Poole himself called "the masses." The enunciation of both these goals appears as early as the first convocation of librarians, held in New York City, almost a quarter of a century before the first American Library Association meeting. There it was in 1853 that Charles Coffin Jewett, then librarian and assistant secretary of the newly formed Smithsonian Institution, delivered his presidential address. "We meet to provide," he said, "for the diffusion of a knowledge of good books, and for enlarging the means of public access to them. Our wishes are for the public, not for ourselves." It was a noble phrase, that diffusion of knowledge, redolent of the writings of great men and great minds and great presidents: the phrase appears in Washington's Farewell Address, was summoned by Jefferson in sponsoring a major educational bill, and was the principal purpose stated in James Smithson's bequest. Jewett proposed to diffuse the knowledge of good books through a national bibliography of all volumes housed in American libraries, a bibliography which was to be printed through the use of stereotyped plates. Envisioning the prospective role of the Smithsonian Institution library, which he defined as the "great central library of reference and research," Jewett proclaimed a bibliothecal new day in which the emerging library profession would not only enjoy the benefits of this great national library but would also participate in the resource sharing that the stereotyped catalog would promote. Visions of this bibliographical richesse dazzled the eyes of that original band of eighty-two delegates, and no less than six resolutions were proposed and adopted commending the Congress, the Smithsonian, and its librarian for their endeavor in support of such important projects. Certainly, no one has ever complained that librarians are reluctant to proffer resolutions, or that they ever were too modest to stake out a claim to national support for their cause.

The story of Professor Jewett's unhappy "mud catalogue" (so-called because to make the plates he used, instead of metal, clay, which subsequently buckled and became unusable) is still remembered affectionately by some librarians, but few will recall that, at that same meeting, another delegate made a proposal of an entirely different order. The Reverend Samuel Osgood, trustee of the Providence Athenaeum, stumped the convention with a plea that the concerns of scholarship should be set aside in favor of the need to spread the popular library movement throughout the land. Not consonant with American democratic goals was any need of rivaling the great libraries of Europe; instead, the delegates should rouse their slumbering townships to the imperative duty of creating popular libraries. And in defense of his position, the Rev. Mr. Osgood offered the following resolution:

> *Resolved,* That while we maintain most decidedly the importance of libraries of the highest class, in furtherance of the most advanced literary and scientific studies, and rejoice in the rise and progress of our few great collections of books for professional scholars, we are convinced that for the present our chief hope must be in the establishment and improvement of *popular* libraries throughout the land.[3]

Thus, even at the beginning, librarians identified two apposite goals: one, the diffusion of knowledge through the highest realms of scholarship; and the other, the nationwide concern for popular literacy and the spread of mass public education.

Almost as a microcosm, that first library convention reflects the macrocosm of the Congressional debates of 1846 over the uses of the Smithson bequest. In his book *American Paradox: The Conflict of Thought and Action,* Merle Curti points to the significance of those debates in crystallizing the opposing views of the eastern Whigs, who favored among other things the establishment of a great research library comparable to that of the British Museum, and of the western Democrats, who urged the foundation of training schools for teachers and the distribution of popularly written tracts. As Robert Dale Owen, Congressman from Indiana, said during those debates:

> To effect permanent good, we must reach the mind and hearts of the masses: we must diffuse knowledge among men; we must not deal it out to scholars and students alone, but even to Tom, Dick, and Harry, and then they will become Mr. Thomas, Mr. Richard, and Mr. Henry.[4]

In their own dialogues the librarians were not quite so blunt; yet even at that first convention of 1853 they proposed a two-pronged approach to library affairs, both of which would be ultimately laid before the seats of government.

By 1876, as I have already noted, Poole was fulminating against the scholarly critics of the new popular libraries, which by then were enjoying the first fruits of local taxation. In his chapter for the Bureau of Education report issued that same year, Poole insisted once again that the public library should not be a library solely for scholars and professional men, but should serve the whole community, mentioning the "mechanic, the laboring man, the sewing-girl, the youth, and all who desire to read, whatever be their rank, intelligence, or condition in life."[5]

Yet, in that same report, in dealing with the topic of college library administration, Otis Robinson, the librarian of the University of Rochester, dealt with the other side of the coin. Having drawn with a broad brush the functions of the society, subscription, and free town libraries, he made this comment:

> Now, a college library is none of these; it is something more than all of them. It is the door to all science, all literature, all art. . . . Well supplied in all its departments, it is a magnificent educational apparatus. How shall the student of to-day become the scholar of to-morrow? It will depend little upon teachers, much about books.[6]

The magnificence of that collegiate educational apparatus leaves much to be conjectured about. Consider that in 1876, Harvard College's collection of 150,000 volumes was already doubled by the holdings of the quite recently founded Boston Public Library; Robinson's library at the University of Rochester housed 12,000 books while Poole's new library in Chicago held over 48,000; the Astor Library of New York had already reached the size of Harvard with over 150,000 volumes, leaving behind the library of Columbia College, which predated the Republic, with rather modest holdings of 18,000 books. In looking at the disparate size of these respective public and academic institutions, one might wonder if those scholars of tomorrow might have done just as well, if not better, grubbing in the educational apparatus provided for their less fortunate brethren: the mechanic, the laboring man, and the sewing-girl. Although the grumblings between the new public librarians and their academic colleagues cast no pall on the official harmonies of that 1876 convention, they must have been there all the same. Buried in a committee report in the *American Library Journal* of the following year is this ominous comment:

> If, however, the college libraries require any special adaption of this movement to themselves—if they have any special wants to be met—their librarians should bestir themselves at once. At present the work is chiefly in the hands of the public libraries.[7]

Clearly, the new profession and its Association began with a dichotomy, and this is reflected even in those early speeches of 1876 which describe the desiderata for the calling of the librarian. If, indeed, the learned libraries required their staffs to have an "indispensable knowledge" of some Latin and Greek, with French, German, Italian, and Spanish thrown in for good measure, the librarians in the new tax-supported institutions defined their requirements in terms of "a courteous disposition which will disclose itself in agreeable manners," noting such qualities as sympathy, cheerfulness, patience, and enthusiasm. I am not suggesting that it was impossible in 1876 for the reader of six languages to have a courteous disposition, but I am suggesting that public and academic librarians viewed themselves and their offices as having very differing orders of magnitude, that a double set of values and aspirations was expressed very early in the American Library Association, that it has been pervasive throughout the history of the Association, and that it continues even today. Indeed, the distinction between the two groups disclosing itself throughout the years could almost serve as a leitmotiv of the professional history of the American librarian.

A random glance at the convention proceedings of any number of years bears out the point. In 1904, when the profession met in St. Louis partly to take advantage of the St. Louis World's Fair and partly to attend the International Congress of Arts and Sciences, where the subject of "the library" was to be made the theme of a principal address, equal-time arrangements had to be made. And two speakers were brought from abroad, one, being the public librarian of Manchester, England, and the other, the librarian of the Royal Laurentian Library in Florence, a research library endowed by Lorenzo the Magnificent. In his own address before ALA that year, Herbert Putnam, then its president, sought to conciliate all parties. Although carefully paying his respects to the world of scholarship, Putnam owned that the problem of library service in the United States was a "peculiar one." "Our task," he said, "is to spread not merely the knowledge of books, but the knowledge of the utility of books. In a democracy of equal liberty and equal opportunity, the education of the citizen is the safety of the state. . . ."[8]

Thus did the concept of the diffusion of knowledge grow; the knowledge of those good books of which Jewett spoke has now become a knowledge of the utility of books. It was, of course, obvious that this democratization of learning was ultimately going to cost quite a great deal of money, and, elsewhere at that 1904 convention, a report was given on "state aid to libraries." The report enunciated the fact that twenty-two states had by that time enacted laws embodying state aid in some form to local public libraries. Of these twenty-two, only ten were making available direct grants-in-aid, while others employed the device of the traveling library. Melvil Dewey, on hearing this news, waxed eloquent: "Libraries have been in a kind of unsettled equilibrium, and we are now coming to the time of centering them on solid foundations, and these foundations are state and national aid."[9]

To return, however, to the growing bifurcation of interests between public and academic libraries, another random example is suggested by the conference of 1905 when the Association met in Portland, Oregon, site of the Lewis and Clark Exposition. President that year was Ernest C. Richardson, librarian of Princeton University. Although specifically asked to speak to the concerns of the popular library in his inaugural address, Richardson opted to remain his own man. Indeed, he had personally received a request from the collegiate librarians of the Pacific Coast to address their needs for more books and resources. Whereas Putnam had noted that the library problem was a "peculiar one," Richardson cited the library problem as a "double one": The problem of the learned library was to furnish all the materials that would aid in the advancement of knowledge; the problem of the popular library, on the other hand, was "to tempt the multitude to read readable books." By now, the uneasy relationship between the collegiate and public librarians was more openly discussed. At that same meeting one speaker addressed the topic of income in the college library:

> Enviously I have been the public librarian, with a city's treasury at his back, wasting his substance in trumpery novels by the thousand. I have pared these college cheese rinds; made home bindings; done double duty to save a salary; stretched the eagle until Uncle Sam would not recognize his proud bird; begged, borrowed (and *almost* stolen) books from reluctant owners.[10]

Thus spoke in 1905 the librarian of the University of California.

By 1933, the year of the Association's conference at the Chicago World's Fair, the double and peculiar problem had become so enmeshed in all of the problems besetting a Depression-ridden profession that President Lydenberg took as the subject of his address the topic "Unanswered Questions." One of those questions was what respite could be offered the library profession when the taxpayer himself needed relief. There were indeed many unanswered questions: The most important was the inequitable distribution of the nation's intellectual wealth and, allied to it, the inequitable manner in which library service was publicly supported. In 1934 the Association moved to adopt a national plan, which Carleton Joeckel described as the "constitution for the library movement." The significance of this step should not be underestimated, for linked with the concept of a nationwide service and a nationwide standard came inevitably the concept of federal aid. Latter-day librarians who think that they have gone through the important meetings wresting old ALA into the twenty-first century would do well to glance back at the early conference years during the 1930s, as the Association debated and then reconciled itself to the idea of direct federal aid. Raised were dire warnings of federal control and of the deadening hand of bureaucracy leveling all library service to mediocrity and uniformity; the debates and arguments fill the pages of the library press.

The trope that runs throughout all the arguments for federal aid was, of course, geography. (Parenthetically, it should be noted that it is no coincidence that Wilson's notable monograph published during the depression years was entitled *The Geography of Reading.*) The United States was perceived as large land mass, in which one-third of the population was not served by any library; in the academic and research areas, the great concentration of library wealth was found to be in the Northeast, along the West Coast, and in certain strategic centers in the Midwest, leaving many sections resource poor. "We have many libraries," the 1934 National Plan commented, "but we do not have a coordinated library system."

From 1904, when ten states were attempting to equalize local tax support for municipal libraries, the grand total by the mid-1930s had inched itself to thirteen. Contemplating whether or not the Association should pursue a policy directed more to the states in furthering the goal of a greater tax base for public libraries, the Association's leaders pushed farther and farther into the direction of federal grants-in-aid. As Joeckel observed: "The great disparity in income and taxpaying ability among the States makes it impossible to establish and maintain an adequate Nationwide minimum standard of library support without recourse to Federal aid."[11] Perhaps this avoidance of the question of state aid for public libraries should be thought of as a missed opportunity. For the states, as

Joeckel clearly perceived, "are the weakest link in the chain of library development." Writing in 1938, he noted that "the proportion of expenditures for library purposes to total State expenditures has declined steadily since 1915. . . ."[12]

Concurrent with the concern for federal aid for the further expansion of public library service was that of the academic librarians for that national bibliographical control, the need of which Jewett had perceived a century ago. Just as the public librarians deployed the WPA funds to launch demonstrations of library service in many rural and unserved portions of the country, so the academic librarians, largely through the aid of WPA-paid employees, inaugurated the great local and regional union catalogs at strategic sites across the country: Philadelphia, Denver, Atlanta, Seattle, Cleveland, and others. "It is safe, I believe," wrote one academic librarian in 1936, "to assume that the ultimate end of union catalog development in the United States is to spread a network of such catalogs over the country, allocated in such a way as to make the necessary materials of scholarly research easily available to each region."[13]

By the mid and late 1930s the profession had progressed beyond debate and developed its own rationale for federal aid, "Libraries and Federal Aid," being the title of the 1936 report of the Association's Special Committee on Federal Aid. Although every type of publicly supported library, including those of the public schools and in state-supported academic institutions, was mentioned as eligible recipients, the report's drafters particularly noted that:

> *Federal grants to the states should be made for the purpose of aiding library service in general, through publicly supported institutions, as contrasted with specific kinds of library service . . .* this recommendation is intended as a warning against the practice of ear-marking federal grants for the exclusive support of special types of libraries. . . .[14]

The bursting of this bibliothecal balloon was not long in coming, as the general-aid-to-education bills, onto which the Association had tacked its library requests, failed repeatedly in the late 1930s of Congressional passage. By the mid-1940s Carl Milam was advocating a policy of retrenchment, and a narrowing of the focus of the library aid program. Especially poignant was his recognition that federal officials did not particularly favor the use of federal funds as an ongoing subsidy to local operations.

> We who deal with foundations have learned that foundation officers like experiments, demonstrations, something new; and that they do not willingly respond to requests for money to provide basic support or to meet deficits. If congressmen are like personal donors or foundation officials—and in many respects they probably are—we may have the answer to our question: Why do we not have federal aid for libraries? Our requests have been, in the main, for basic support. They were logical enough, but not particularly stirring. It is necessary to admit that I have not produced a formula which meets these specifications.[15]

Narrowing its focus to the rural public library movement, the Association finally realized through its lobbying efforts the passage in 1956 of the Library Services Act. By the mid-1960s, almost all types of libraries had become involved, federal legislation making eligible the libraries of public schools and academic institutions. In addition, the public library law was amended to include all public libraries regardless of size.

And what was the rationale for this federal support by type of library? It was presumably equality. As early as 1938 Joeckel, in his report for President Roosevelt's Advisory Committee on Education, had written: "The central theme of this brief survey of American libraries has been inequality. The book resources of the Nation are at least as unevenly distributed as are its economic resources." And of what did the inequality consist? The librarians perceived the inequities between urban and rural libraries, between sections and regions of the country, and between the fulfillment of the needs of the researcher and those of the ordinary citizen.

Just as Jewett had probed the writings of Presidents to take for the new profession the ideal of a diffusion of knowledge, so now the librarians adopted the stirring governmental mandate: equality of educational opportunity, a phrase that gained prominence in Roosevelt's Administration and which has since been invoked at all levels of government and used by both educators and the lay public alike. In its historic decision *Brown* v. *Board of Education,* the Supreme Court used it to invoke precedence for the integration of the public schools; President Johnson used it when he instituted among his Great Society programs the nation's first massive federal aid to public elementary and secondary schools; and the Congress used it when it mandated under the aegis of the Civil Rights Act a study to be commissioned analyzing the "equalization of educational opportunity," a study popularly known as the Coleman report. And what were the inequities that all of this massive judicial, administrative, and legislative program was designed to eradicate? They were very grave, and they had existed for a very long time; the inequities that all three branches of the government perceived ripe for eradication were those which divided the races, shut out the poor, and isolated from the cultural and economic mainstream the non-nativist American. Thus, government identified the ethnic, racial, and economic minority groups.

And government did not propose to eradicate these inequities through parity or institutional aid but took instead the path of compensation for people. The children of low-income families were to be the target of federal aid through Title I of the Elementary and Secondary Education Act. Even today the administrative unit to which this program is assigned in the Executive Branch is known as the Division of Compensatory Education. Far from dropping grants-in-aid indiscriminately on all students or on all academic institutions, the legislation of the Higher Education Act specified educational opportunity grants for students "of exceptional financial need" and nominated for remedial funding new and developing institutions, such as black or community colleges. And what do the librarians have as their federal legislative programs? They have programs of parity: every academic institution receives a basic grant of $5,000 regardless of the fact that some institutions expend upwards of $1,000,000 for their resources while others cannot even match the sum of $5,000 because their budgets are less than that amount. The federal aid program to public libraries consists of a basic floor of $200,000 for each state, and makes available the remainder of the appropriation on a per capita basis, taking into account no index of state effort nor state wealth nor per capita income. And this at a time when still approximately one-third of the states do not have a state-aid program, although federal pump-priming designed to elicit state-aid response has been going on for two decades. And the question remains, how does one equalize when all are presumed equal?

Just as Jewett faced his own problems convincing a reluctant government that the diffusion of knowledge required a universal catalog of all books housed in American libraries, so, too, the librarians of today face no less a battle in convincing the Administration that their programs of parity truly reduce the inequities of educational opportunity. If the "equal chance," as used by the library profession in the 1940s had any real meaning, it was appropriate to that first foray librarians made to seek federal aid, when indeed the rural unserved poor were to receive the benefits accorded those served by municipal libraries, the latter then ineligible for federal aid. Once that distinction was lost, the legislated programs for libraries partook too much of the concept that there should be something for everybody.

But, and I anticipate the arguments already, Congress supported the library programs; it makes the laws. It is true that Congress makes the law. Yet, nearly every major piece of social-action legislation in this country since Franklin D. Roosevelt's Administration has been hatched in the Executive Office of the President, an office which Roosevelt himself created by executive order. From WPA to ESEA, and from Social Security to MEDICARE, many major social legislative programs, although introduced by Congress, modified by it, and enacted by it, emanated from the White House. Library legislation, with an exception or so, does not partake of this pattern; it has for the most part remained outside the mainstream of Presidential and executive-branch endorsement. Federal budget cuts in library programs, it should be remembered, did not begin with the Nixon Administration.

At present, the library programs occupy a kind of half-way house, supported by some members of Congress and begrudgingly funded when pushed to the wall by the Administration. That the recommendation to terminate the library programs suggested by the Nixon Administration in fiscal 1974 should have been so surprising to everyone is in itself a puzzlement. Since Herbert Hoover's day, the Republican party has maintained a significant posture of not supporting categorical grants-in-aid. From 1965 to 1967, at the time of the librarian's greatest Congressional victories, over fifty bills were introduced into Congress endorsing revenue sharing by some 57 Congressional sponsors or cosponsors, and 45 of the sponsors were members of the Republican party. Melvín Laird, at that time Chairman of the House Republican conference and a long-time advocate of federal tax-sharing, openly criticized the whole concept of categorical aid as "the second best method of attacking the problems in our society" and extolled revenue sharing as the "great Republican alternative to the Great Planned Society."

Yet, it would be unfair to characterize the whole demise of the library categorical-aid programs as a maneuver of the Republican party. There are other reasons, most pertinently that which Daniel Patrick Moynihan has termed the cycle of denial and diminishing returns:

> Public services follow production functions as do any other production processes. Typically, in an early state increments of input have a high marginal utility which gradually diminishes until the exchange of input for output is no longer equal, and finally to the point where additional input is almost totally wasted as virtually no additional output results. . . . The early and exhilarating days of large increments of output for small increments of input are long past. In these circumstances "trying harder" has no discernible effect, and a perverse equilibrium is attained, at least from the point of view of those whose pleasure or profit it is to demand more. No matter how hard the polity tries to produce "more," it never does, so that the posture of demanding more is never endangered by the prospect of fulfillment. Education would seem to be a preeminent instance of this phenomenon. . . . A shoe factory operating in the manner of many public school systems would have long since closed down.[16]

In this regard, the federally legislated library programs have much in common with the phenomenon which Moynihan describes. How exhilarated the library profession was by that modest program of 1956, which launched all of $2,050,000 into the library world. There was an example of a little input which wrought quite a sizable output. Somehow, during the intervening years, that "seed-money program" has now grown to the proportions of the "federal share." It is not only the government which has changed and modified its policies; the Association has also greatly modified its own.

And, now, in the midst of what have been discouraging years, comes a new suggestion that the libraries of the Bicentennial nation should become a part of a nationwide network, conjoined by computers and telecommunications, to further equalize access to books and materials. Indeed, the very first page of the preface announcing this concept uses the word "new" four times. I am a little uncertain, but I believe that it was Chaucer who said that there was nothing new under the sun, and Chaucer was, of course, quoting Ecclesiastes. I suggest that the application of technology to library affairs is not anything new, and that the library dream of perfecting a technique to unify library service nationwide is really quite old. Jewett dreamed with the stereotyped plates; Wallace, who gave the keynote address in 1876, the year that the duplex telegraph was exhibited during the Centennial Exposition, believed that the telegraph might provide assistance to the work of the librarian. Writing in 1883, Charles A. Cutter, in predicting the future, held out for the accumulation of phonographic reproductions of rare books, which could be read off "through the wires to the end of the Union. All the libraries in the country, you see," he wrote, "are practically one library."[17] Justin Winsor, in 1894, in speaking of Franklin's contribution in founding the Philadelphia library, noted: "When he tamed the lightning, we may yet see what he rendered possible through electricity for library administration. . . . We don't know what will come of the phonograph," Winsor added, ". . . I look to see its marvellous capacities yet utilized in the service of the librarian."[18] Addressing the librarians at that 1904 meeting in St. Louis, Guido Biagi, the Italian research librarian, prefigured that:

. . . the day will come when the libraries of Europe and of America and of all the states in the Postal Union will form, as it were, one single collection, and the old books, printed when America was but a myth, will enter new worlds bearing with them to far off students the benefit of their ancient wisdom. The electric post of the airships will have then shortened distances, the telephone will make it possible to hear at Melbourne a graphophone disc asked for, a few minutes earlier, from the British Museum. There will be few readers, but an infinite number of hearers, who will listen from their own homes to the spoken paper, to the spoken book.[19]

In 1938 Frederick Keppel, president of the Carnegie Corporation of New York, permitted himself a fantasy in looking forward; in that Utopian future he pretended to look back, and wrote, "Last week we were in touch through the Interlingual Clearing House at Geneva with a biophysicist in Tirana and an anthropologist in Peking, both of whom were glad to give us what we needed."[20]

In 1951 Charles Armstrong, in his report on library finances for the Public Library Inquiry, made note of the possibility of a research library network, providing a reference service to serious researchers using highly specialized materials at any point in the country where a public library unit exists. Because, he added, of its essentially nonlocal and interstate character the reference network might appropriately be supported by the federal government. And in 1961, the historian Lewis Mumford in his book *The City in History* described the framework of the new "invisible" city in terms of a functional grid or network having capacities for "swift transportation, mechanical manifolding, electronic transmission, world-wide distribution." In the technological sphere, he gave as his example the electric power grid, a network of relatively independent power stations which, when linked together, provide a greater flexibility and security than would be possible from any one of the individual parts of the system. In the cultural area Mumford described the national library loan system in England, through which a reader's request for a specific title not available in his own library is successively transmitted through a hierarchy of larger regional libraries to be filled. If this fails, appeal is made to the London center which has command of all the libraries within the cultural network. "With both the electric power grid and the library loan system, the largest facilities become available, not by heaping them together, but by articulating them into a system that enables the individual user, provided he uses an organized unit in the local area, to switch on this or that resource as needed."[21] Mumford concluded the chapter by noting that this new order of both cultural and electronic diffusion had been perceived a century ago by Emerson, and he cited from Emerson's writing this observation: "Our civilization and these ideas are reducing the earth to a brain. See how by telegraph and steam the earth is anthropolized."

And so in the century of Emerson and of Jewett, the century which witnessed the invention of the telegraph and the first application of steam to the process of printing itself, the story of the library network really begins. Tape drives whirling away with capacity for rapid access to the world's knowledge may indeed be the latest of the technological innovations, but the concept of the United States as a nation of multiple library jurisdictions but with a single bibliographical base is really, considering the age of the nation, quite old. In each decade, whether it was through stereotyped printing, or telegraphic or telephonic communications, or the invention of the phonographic recording, or the microreduction of alphanumeric characters on cinema film, the library profession has discovered that the new technologies could not only be used, in Winsor's phrase, "in the service of the librarian," but could also be applied to that elusive concept of many parts forming a whole. The computer is but the latest of these new technologies.

Yet, all of this is not to say that there is nothing new in the new National Program. Its real novelty lies in the fusion of the aims and clienteles which this profession has long held to be of two kinds. Let me recall for you what I noted at the beginning that Poole believed that the public library should serve the "mechanic, the laboring man, the sewing-girl, the youth, and all who desire to read, whatever be their rank, intelligence, or condition in life." Conversely, the librarian of the University of Rochester made it clear that the collegiate library was directed toward the scholars of tomorrow. And ever since that initial gathering those two types of libraries were perceived so distinctly that presidents of the Association were only able to focus their remarks about the "double" problem of library service.

But in its first draft, the National Commission on Libraries and Information Science defined the purpose of a national network as affording the opportunity to any citizen "be he a businessman, researcher, scholar, or student—in the public or private sector" to have access to the total knowledge resource of the country from his own physical location.[22] Herein lies the novelty: that the bibliographical resources of all libraries should be accessible not only to those scholars of tomorrow but also to all who desire to read—whatever be their rank, intelligence, or condition in life. In this matter, which relates to the history of ideas, the Commission's proposal places within one context the dual philosophies of the profession, and within a single service ideal combines the disparate aims of the public and academic librarian. In a rhetorical sense, it is as if someone over the course of the years finally realized that the magnificent national educational apparatus of the United States should also be the heritage of the mechanic, laboring man, sewing-girl, and youth. The goal of the diffusion of knowledge, which Jewett perceived lay in the matter of national bibliographical control, is now closer to the equalization of educational opportunity, both of them aims of this profession, both of them phrases culled from the writings of Presidents, and both of them aspirations consonant with the life of the mind in America. Yet in tying these two goals together, and in assimilating as one the client groups of those so long divided constituencies, the Commission's proposed solution could only alleviate the geographical distribution of the nation's intellectual wealth. It does not have the capacity to address those governmentally perceived inequities of racial, cultural, educational, or economic isolation and disadvantagement. I believe that the Commission itself perceives this, and so my remarks are not meant to be unduly insensitive or critical of its work or worth.

But perhaps it is time to suggest that the Association and the profession move away from the trope of geography, and relate the needs for continued federal aid for their client groups not solely to regional or sectional disparities in the matter of intellectual wealth but to personal economic and social disparities.

This is by no means an easy task, or one which should solely be the responsibility of the federal government. With several brilliant exceptions, the record of library support by the states is still not very significant. It is my hope that the state-level conferences to be supported by the proposed White House Conference on Libraries will devote considerable attention to the role of the state in the equalization of local tax support for public libraries. In all but one state, Vermont, State Commissions on School Library Finance have been established, and a comparable mechanism is very much needed to address the questions of local tax-supported libraries. At present, over 40 percent of the tax revenues supporting the public schools is derived from state taxation; the percentage for libraries derived from state tax coffers is less than 12 percent. Closing this gap is a task for the future, and one that in the past the Association, although acknowledging it, has not significantly addressed.

This action, however, will not diminish the future work of the Association in seeking further federal aid. I offer only a few recommendations in this matter for your consideration. First, I would like to suggest that the Association put forth its program in terms of client, not institutional, needs. Federal policy-makers are not as sympathetic to saving the nation's libraries as they are to saving the nation's children and its youth and to alleviating some of the burdens of the nation's old. The present legislated library programs seem greatly geared to the requirements of the library, but they have not the specificity of other federal educational programs in defining the requirements of the client group, whether it be children of low-income parents or students of exceptional financial need. Second, and I suspect this is a recommendation that probably will never be implemented, I would like to see greater cohesion in the Association's position, one that might perhaps convey the solidity of the Association and not every one of its different divisions and units. I realize that aid to public libraries does little for the college library, and that aid to the public schools provides no succor for the nation's public libraries, but at the same time so small a profession with so many claimants to the public purse achieves in the end fairly small pockets of support which, when dispersed, seem fiscally insignificant. In fiscal 1941 when WPA funds were used to support employees working in public libraries, the amount per capita amounted to 13 cents. In fiscal 1971, thirty years later, the per capita amount under Title I of LSCA amounted to 17 cents. This very fiscal insignificance gives rise to the suspicion, whether totally warranted or not, that federal aid to libraries could be reduced or terminated without too much difficulty. And governmental decision makers do look into federal funding on per capita bases. Even a simple legislative change, such as making available public library funds on a per capita basis of income rather than mere population, could appear more responsive to the equalization principle enunciated by previous Administrations.

And last, I would like to mention an important need that very few people in the Association have recognized, and that is the great responsibility for the library profession to call for in its behalf what is commonly called policy research. Policy research is research proposed and carried out to aid the government in its own decision making. It is true that the Commission could indeed carry out this mission, but its funds are still limited, and would not at this time support studies of the magnitude of Coleman's research, surely one of the most formidable policy-research documents yet mandated by Congress. I stress this, also, because I believe members of the Association have shown relatively little interest in the need to continue the federal funds which could support such research, now mandated by the Higher Education Act, Title II-B. I would make these a first-priority concern. As a profession, you have not pursued the course of policy research, and I do not recall that any article in a professional library journal has ever described it. Yet, policy research, about which there is a large literature in other fields, is intended not as a contribution to the discipline or to the profession but rather as a contribution and guide to governance itself. Just as one example, almost all major studies dealing with the property tax question as it affects the finance of the schools and as it is affected by the rulings of the Supreme Court are examples of policy research studies, and a goodly number of them are funded by the federal government itself.

I know that many groups and units in the Association are now at work on revisions of the present federal legislative pattern. Naturally, all of us have now the benefit of hindsight, but changing the dimensions of our federal legislative programs will not in any way denigrate or deny the strength of purpose and dedication with which the Association's first attempts at federal aid were carried out. Times have a way of changing, and it is in your look to the future that you must be responsive to differing aspects of the social and political climates of our times. In conclusion, I should just like to say that the look that all of us will have to take

> . . . will have to be forward to the new and unfamiliar. Legislation will have to be formulated to meet new needs. Financial support will require broader bases. Cooperation will have to assume varied forms. Measurement of library service and training for librarianship will have to be adjusted to new conditions and related to a frame of reference which will illuminate, which will justify, and which will vitalize the work of the library as an American social institution of fundamental importance and worth.[23]

I wish I could claim such a peroration to be mine. But those last few lines about the new and unfamiliar are quoted from the inaugural address of Louis Round Wilson at the ALA Conference of 1936. And so I come to the last of the paradoxes: in one sense, nothing changes but change itself.

REFERENCES

1. Salome Cutler Fairchild, "Women in American Libraries," *Library Journal*, 29: C157 (Dec. 1904).

2. William Frederick Poole, "Some Popular Objections to Public Libraries," *American Library Journal*, 1: 50 (Nov. 30, 1876).

3. Samuel Osgood, "Popular Libraries," in George Burwell Utley, *The Librarian's Conference of 1853* (Chicago: American Library Association, 1951), p. 156.

4. Quoted in Merle Curti, *American Paradox: The Conflict of Thought and Action* (New Brunswick, N.J.: Rutgers University Press, 1956), p. 35.

5. U.S. Bureau of Education, *Public Libraries of the United States of America: Their History, Condition, and Management; Special Report,* Part I (Washington: Government Printing Office, 1876), p. 477.

6. Ibid., p. 506.

7. Otis H. Robinson, et al., "Co-operative College Cataloguing," *American Library Journal,* 1: 435 (Aug. 31, 1877).

8. Herbert Putnam, "Address of the President," *Library Journal,* 29: C26 (Dec. 1904).

9. Melvil Dewey, ["Discussion of Miss Countryman's Paper"], *Library Journal,* 29: C212 (Dec. 1904).

10. Joseph C. Rowell, "On the Distribution of Income in the College Library," *Library Journal,* 30: C84–85 (Sept. 1905).

11. Carleton B. Joeckel, *Library Service* (Washington: Government Printing Office, 1938), p. 76.

12. Ibid., p. 20.

13. Donald Coney, "The Union Catalog: Its Future," *Bulletin of the American Library Association,* 30: 542 (July 1936).

14. American Library Association, Special Committee on Federal Aid, "Libraries and Federal Aid," *Bulletin of the American Library Association,* 30: 456 (May 1936, Pt. II).

15. Carl H. Milam, "Federal Aid to Libraries," in Carleton B. Joeckel, ed., *Library Extension* (Chicago: University of Chicago Press, 1946), p. 227.

16. Daniel P. Moynihan, *Coping: On the Practice of Government* (New York: Vintage Books, 1975), pp. 382–83.

17. Charles A. Cutter, "The Buffalo Public Library in 1983," *Library Journal* 8: 216 (Sept.-Oct. 1883).

18. Justin Winsor, "The Development of the Library," *Library Journal,* 19: 372–73 (Nov. 1894).

19. Guido Biagi, "The Library: Its Past and Future," *Library Journal,* 29: C12 (Dec. 1904).

20. Frederick Keppel, "Looking Forward, A Fantasy," in Emily Miller Danton, ed., *The Library of Tomorrow: A Symposium* (Chicago: American Library Association, 1939), p. 8.

21. Lewis Mumford, *The City in History* (New York: Harcourt, Brace & World, Inc., 1961), p. 566.

22. U.S. National Commission on Libraries and Information Science, *A New National Program of Library and Information Service* (Washington, D.C., 1973), p. 4.

23. Louis Round Wilson, "Restudying the Library Chart," *Bulletin of the American Library Association,* 30: 490 (June 1936).

Herman Liebaers

Grand Marshal to the Court of Belgium

Mr. Liebaers also served as Royal Librarian of Belgium from 1956 to 1973 and as President of the International Federation of Library Associations from 1969 to 1974.

He was presented the highest award of the American Library Association, Honorary Membership, on July 19, 1976, during the Centennial Conference in Chicago. The citation presented to him reads in part:

You were central in making the national library [of Belgium] a powerful instrument of modern scholarship, cultural growth, and bibliographic service: a distinguished exemplar among the great learned libraries of the world. . . .

Throughout your career, you have been a perceptive missionary for better understanding between our two countries, . . . as a Fellow and Associate Secretary of the Belgian American Educational Foundation and as a consultant to the Council on Library Resources. . . .

For your powerful and forthright contribution in the highest councils of professional librarianship throughout the world the ALA . . . grants you its highest award.

THE IMPACT OF AMERICAN AND EUROPEAN
LIBRARIANSHIP UPON EACH OTHER

MAY I START with what the French call *une précaution oratoire,* an informal warning: No extensive research went into this paper, but it is based on a lifelong experience, the better part of which was devoted to international cooperation. I have been too much of an actor, too little of a detached observer.

Shortly after I entered the profession, close to the end of World War II, a senior colleague told me a story of four young American librarians who had reorganized the old Vatican library. For a long time I believed that it was a joke to oppose a dynamic American counterculture to the static wisdom embedded in a centuries-old collection of secular and religious manuscripts. When I realized that the story was true, I faced at once a problem which has never left me since—library techniques versus subject knowledge. Time and again this tension turned up when I tried to compare American and European librarianship. Over the years I have expressed it in many different ways. If I remember one of the better ones, I would say in retrospect what I said about five or six years ago on the occasion of the dedication of a new library building at UCLA: "In Europe, the libraries are better than the librarians," sternly refusing to add the expected second part of the sentence. The fact that one day I would dedicate a new American library could not have occurred to me when I entered the profession, but if it had, I would have considered it to be a joke like that of the young American librarians reorganizing the Vatican library.

You should know that I never had any formal library training, as is the case still today with nearly all librarians from the European continent working in research libraries. The only relationship of these librarians with formal training is that they nearly all teach in library schools at the sub-university level. I committed the same sin, but only for a short time. I even had to look up my poorly kept archives to see what course I gave. Also like these other librarians I had an academic training. In my case it was Dutch poetry of the nineteenth century. This subject was never of any use in my professional work, but the training it supplied has always been an invaluable asset. So you will easily understand that professional training, in the sense that you use the word, has not the same importance in my thinking as it does in yours. It is one of the advantages of comparative librarianship that it forces one to question the automaticity of priorities.

I started this paper with the direct question of library techniques versus subject knowledge because it has been my life's experience that you need a few ideas—they may even be preconceived ideas—to face the reality of the surrounding world. This reality being a library, the complexity of the relationship between form and content, between library technique and subject knowledge, between typography and literary quality represents one such idea. Modern linguistics has given a new dimension to the distinction the old antinomy made between *le contenant et le contenu*. I guess that such a need for fixed ideas is what was called in the nineteenth century a philosophy of life. For me this has also meant a never-ending crossing of the ocean to try to understand on both sides the roots and the flowers of the professional trees. In my contacts with American librarianship, the Library of Congress came before ALA. My love affair with the Library of Congress started more than a quarter of a century ago. That was when the Librarian of Congress issued a notice saying that some false rumours were spread that he was going to accept an important international appointment. His name was Luther H. Evans, soon to become director-general of UNESCO.

Early in 1951 I was appointed consultant at LC for a six weeks' period, which allowed me to say, until two years ago, at every reception in the Whittall Pavilion, that I was the oldest staff member, each time, however, being corrected by Walter Ristow, who protested, rightly, that he was the oldest one. He is now retired, but I am too in a certain way. This is not just an anecdote. It indicates one of the aspects of American librarianship which frequently strikes me: the turnover of the staff and its mobility.

In Europe, more particularly in the Latin part of Europe, something is wrong with you if you change from one library to another. In the United States, something is wrong with you if you do not change. I stayed for thirty years in the same library, and when I left it was not for another library. After a long period of observation, I would be tempted to conclude that both traditions have more weaknesses than advantages. These diverging traditions are, of course, not limited to the library field but belong to two different forms of society. This is one of my other *idées fixes*: A community has the library it deserves and the library has the staff it deserves. That is, of course, not completely true, but it nearly is.

The difference between the two traditions, however, is not as sharp today as it was twenty-five years ago. International cooperation has something to do with this change, but we should not exaggerate its impact. When the American Memorial Library was built in Berlin immediately after World War II, as a symbol of democratic freedom opposed to the recent Nazi nightmare, it was gradually turned into a good German public library concept. No harm in that—quite the contrary. It is better that international cooperation bends slightly in the direction of the national environment, rather than being left at the neutral level of grandiloquent speeches about peace and so on.

After my consultantship at the Library of Congress was over, my admiration for American librarianship began. During my first stay in the United States, I visited one hundred libraries in three months, and I would never do that again. This may explain why in later years I always said that I preferred librarians to libraries. Actually my order of preference early in my career was: libraries, books, librarians. In later years it changed into: librarians, books, libraries.

Though I spent a few days in Chicago in 1951, I did not visit the ALA headquarters and I did not meet the newly appointed executive director, David Clift, who became later a good friend. The reason was very simple: I did not know of the existence of ALA. I guess I have to apologize, but it's the truth. In the United States the librarians I met in 1951 hardly had time to talk about their own libraries, and when the shoptalk was over, they questioned me about Europe, not about libraries in Europe, but about that old continent with its idiosyncrasies which they liked so much. In my home country I was a nonactive member of a library association which meant nothing to the profession. Still today many library associations in Europe, and once again I must stress more particularly in the Latin part of Europe, do not mean much to the profession.

Some years ago I said that the British Library Association has twenty thousand members and the French association two hundred. The two figures are wrong, but the difference is correct! In countries like France and Belgium where the government does everything or pretends to do everything, library associations look more like learned societies. The members listen to a scholarly paper about an unknown manuscript and the closest they come to matters of professional interest is in the description of bibliographical ghosts. Many of these associations bring together librarians and archivists, the latter often being the more active members. I developed a theory that in those countries where archivists and librarians were members of the same association, the libraries were in a state of underdevelopment. I was never very popular among archivists, but I am still not convinced that I might have been wrong.

IFLA, the International Federation of Library Associations, introduced ALA to me, though the relationship between the two organizations existed long before I was aware of it. I would like to recall my first acquaintance with ALA because I think it is rather typical for a number of European librarians. It was at an IFLA General Council meeting in Madrid in 1958 that, during a trip to the Escurial, Douglas Bryant introduced me to John Cory and Jack Dalton. Douglas Bryant had just finished his term on IFLA's Executive Board and Jack Dalton was taking over. The latter was still sitting on the Board when I became a member in Rome in 1964. It was, however, with Foster Mohrhardt, a former ALA president, who joined the Board in 1965, that I had the longest association.

I was surprised to discover that these American Board members got their travel expenses paid by their library association. In my part of Europe we always had to rely on government funds. I gradually began to realize that library associations were important for the development of the profession, both nationally and internationally. Moreover, these col-

leagues from the New World were highly qualified and had an open-
mindedness toward the world at large that strongly impressed me. What
I also discovered with some surprise was that they were the only members
of the Board who reported home about the IFLA Board meetings. They
came to the meetings well prepared, with or without instructions, and
their remarks were always a bit more formal but much more to the point
than ours. At the time I did not know that international commitments
were a point of issue within ALA, as is the case again today, unfortu-
nately, as I understand it. I simply thought that ALA naturally owed its
cooperation to IFLA because of the high degree of development of American librarianship. I would like to add a footnote to this recollection of my
first encounter with American librarians outside the United States. All of
them were perfect ambassadors of their native country abroad. This is a
positive way to introduce a negative remark: Over the years I have met
many outstanding American librarians who lost all their qualities and
qualifications once they were outside their home country. I am not referring at all or hardly at all to their pronunciation of the English language,
but to their basic mistake, which was to assume that the institutional
framework, within which one had to work, was American all over the
world. Some of these librarians, who were to fail in their missions abroad,
never realized that the simple word "library" had a different meaning
along the shores of the Potomac than along the Seine, not to mention the
Ganges. This would probably also be true of other than American peaceful
conquerors of the world, but I did not meet them, except for a couple of
my French or British friends.

Actually, ALA was present at the very inception of IFLA. This happened
half a century ago and the details of the story have been written down
elsewhere. Next year, on the occasion of the fiftieth anniversary of IFLA,
it will receive full treatment again. May it suffice to say here that this
early cooperation between American and European professional organizations is typical of the development of international nongovernmental organizations. Just as the adherence of the socialist countries in the fifties
and of the developing countries in the seventies is reflecting a general
trend in transnational cooperation. Notwithstanding its name, IFLA was

for a long time not exactly an international organization, but much more of a European-American venture. In the early history of IFLA, ALA contributed a president, William W. Bishop, a leading librarian of his day and chairman of ALA's International Relations Committee. He had no American successor, however, just as the limited IFLA meeting in Chicago in 1933 was unique until the recent General Council meeting in Washington in 1974. Thirty-five participated in 1933, one thousand in 1974. There was a depression in 1933, an economic decline in 1974. Besides William W. Bishop and Carl H. Milam, executive secretary of ALA, one or two other American librarians appear on the lists of participants in the early meetings in Europe. The preponderance of Europeans was obvious. Each year a small group of American librarians crossed the ocean, and glancing through the IFLA proceedings of those years, one cannot avoid the feeling that they were the happy few who could afford a return to the sources, as we say in French. In those days—that means until the outbreak of World War II—IFLA was no professional international organization, but rather a distinguished gentlemen's club, where old friends, who happened to be librarians, talked for a few days every year, at the invitation of one of them, about matters of common interest, and had a good time. This image of IFLA was revived after the war in 1947 and I would not pretend that all its features are gone today. This is a period in the history of European-American library cooperation which I have termed amateurish. We were professionals in our libraries, in our national library organizations, at least in some Anglo-Saxon countries or countries which developed under their influence, but we stepped down to the amateur level in reaching the international scene. Effective results of this form of cooperation are difficult to detect, but it undoubtedly paved the way for the multilateral stream of ideas and programs with which we are familiar today.

From this vantage point it is strange to read again the welcoming speech with which William W. Bishop addressed the European guests in Chicago in 1933. It sounds like the incunabulum era of international cooperation. "I should like to dwell briefly," said Bishop, "on some conditions and characteristics of American library development which I find all too frequently unfamiliar to my European colleagues."

The use of the term "public" libraries allowed him to stress the fact of the historic division of the United States into quasi-independent states, and "an even more marked centrifugal divorce of our cities and counties from our State governments, as well as from national, Federal control. Local public opinion is in the end the only driving force compelling the establishment and support of such means of both culture and education as schools, libraries, museums and galleries of art." However, he adds rightly, "It would be wholly unbecoming in this connection to fail to point out the enormous practical assistance to all American libraries of the work of the Library of Congress, an assistance, however, based on voluntary cooperation and in no way upon control or direction." And then follows a nearly prophetic remark: "To me the power of this conception—that means of individual service which the research libraries have taken over from the public libraries—of library service in the American scientific libraries holds out great promise for the future. If once we can come through this trying financial crisis, with our ideals of service unimpaired, we shall go forward to a development of mechanical apparatus, of mutual aid, of cooperative efforts in all directions which will enable us to use to the full the books we have spent so much time and money in gathering." In passing he gives tribute to the special libraries and their Association "in spite of the greatest possible diversity of interest and of subject matter in its constituent librarians and libraries."

William W. Bishop ends with a laudatory presentation of ALA to the European members of his audience. "Without ALA librarianship in America would today have stood on a far lower plane," but I do not feel it to be my duty here today to quote at length from these compliments.

Within the last few years, though, the pattern of cooperation has changed drastically. ALA is no longer alone in the United States in its approach to the international library community. Other American IFLA member-associations are the Music Library Association, the American Association of Law Libraries, the Medical Library Association, the Art Libraries Association, and the Association of Research Libraries; there are also 112 institutional members. SLA, it is worth noting, had already invited foreign librarians to a dinner party during the 1933 Chicago session.

But IFLA also is no longer alone. Actually, it has never been, because the International Federation for Documentation is a much older organization with similar interests, to which I shall come back in a few moments. But the main factor of change, for better or for worse, is the existence of UNESCO. The prewar International Institute of Intellectual Cooperation never meant for the international dimension of our profession what UNESCO now means. In other words, governmental influence has never been as powerful as nowadays, both at the national and the international levels. This induced me to say at the opening of the fortieth General Council in Washington (1974), "Let's be aware of the danger that politics and profession may appear in the wrong order of importance, let us avoid to put at the top what belongs at the bottom and vice versa." May I use the opportunity which is offered to me here today, before such a large audience, to appeal to individual ALA members to participate actively in international cooperation. The strength of international nongovernmental organizations, such as IFLA, will guarantee automatically the eminence of the profession over politics and will gradually counterbalance an international community of governments with an international community of people.

In my following comments I may be biased toward ALA and IFLA, and this may even be unfair to other national and international organizations, both governmental and nongovernmental, but the general trend of my thinking will remain close, at least I hope so, to the reality of international cooperation.

After World War II, ALA stepped boldly outside the borders of the United States through an enhanced program of its International Relations Office. In the David Clift *Festschrift* issue of *American Libraries* (July-August 1972), Emerson Greenaway contributes an excellent paper on "Progress in International Librarianship." I would like to quote somewhat at random:

> *Education of Librarians.* Emphasis was rightly given to education for librarianship and most of this activity centered in Asian countries. The U.S. Department of State provided funds for two projects to *provide* library school study and in-service training for nine

Indian university librarians. The University of Delhi received fiscal
support in the expansion and development of its program of library education from the Rockefeller Foundation. This same Foundation aided also in the strengthening of the Japan library school
at Keio University; assistance in the development of a graduate
program of library education at the University of the Philippines;
and the establishment of a library school at the National Taiwan
University. In the Middle East, the Ford Foundation assisted in the
establishment of a library education program at the University of
Ankara.

On reading this paragraph, however, I could not avoid noting that all
of the countries mentioned—not the "institutions" as such—still lack a de-
cent library system and have hardly any interest in international cooperation. Take India, for example, still struggling with that nonsensical legacy
of the British Empire, with its national library in Calcutta. There is no
generally representative library association, but instead a series of com-
peting state library associations, the whole purpose of which seems to be
an occasional meeting at which invited "messages" from abroad are read.
In most university libraries, three parallel classification systems exist. The
ghost of Ranganathan is still floundering around. Japan is another case at
hand: An isolated Library of Congress, called the Diet Library, refusing
or accepting very reluctantly to take national leadership, and a Japan Library Association behaving like a group of librarians from a developing
country. If one compares the strong international impact of Japanese
publishers with the lack of international interest on the part of Japanese
librarians, it is almost a shame for our profession. This truth is even
sadder when one realizes the intensity of the professional traffic between
the United States and Japan over the years.
  I could go on, but it seems to me more useful to look for an explanation.
In my humble opinion—as people in the East say when they have not the
slightest reservation about their opinion—the problem is not the old one
of whether it is more profitable to send librarians abroad for training or
to receive at home professional teachers from abroad. This seems to me to
be a false problem. There is enough experience gained so that we can agree

on the efficiency of undergraduate training at home and graduate training abroad, with, of course, a number of exceptions, as with all general rules. I would not press again the point that training as such may probably not be the best answer. What I want to stress is that library development relies on the quality of a limited number of persons, in developed as well as in developing countries. The only difference between the two types of countries is that in the latter these men or women are far too rare. If you have such a man, let's say, in Malaysia, he will feel the need to travel to the United States, to Europe, and to Japan, to be exposed to different library experiences, to talk to the few librarians from whom he can learn the strategy of selling the library idea at home, because the major problem is to convince local and national authorities of the genuine library solution that has to be given in particular circumstances. This requires a high degree of professional experience, intellectual power, and strong character. Not many people combine these qualities, in or outside the library profession.

Governments are not good at finding such persons or even at recognizing them when they present themselves, which happens sometimes. And here I have a first but sharp criticism to address to an intergovernmental organization like UNESCO. I think I can speak with some authority about UNESCO: For over a period of fifteen years, I have been sent by UNESCO to developing countries, mainly in Asia, on short assignments, and I have been for many years a member of UNESCO's International Advisory Committee on Documentation, Libraries and Archives. Service to UNESCO is extremely frustrating. The Secretariat—these are the officials in Paris—live in a world apart. Generally they are not chosen for their competence, but by a criterion of geographical distribution that is, in fact, political distribution. This is unavoidable in the world in which we live, but people chosen in that way should at least be modest when they meet us, the professionals. The contrary is the case. In a language which is not always understandable they build up a theoretical framework, which is just empire building of one UNESCO division against another, in which they try to encompass some of the ideas they may have picked up when they happened to be listening to us.

This is, in turn, no theoretical attack. I shall give you two examples. They may seem to lead me away from my subject, but I think that they will show rather well the reality of international cooperation: UNISIST and Universal Bibliographic Control. Let me, however, repeat once more—and very explicitly—that international cooperation is worth all the troubles. It enriches everyone, even those who never had the opportunity to participate directly in cosmopolitan forums.

UNISIST is a brilliant example of successful international maneuvering. A couple of clever people at the International Council of Scientific Unions–Abstracting Board realized that the science information division of UNESCO had a very weak program and proposed to them to reinvent the wheel. The acronym UNISIST stands for a world science information system. Each generation has had its UNISIST but under another name. I know one of the pre-UNISISTs rather well because it was launched in my native city of Brussels under the title *Institut International de Bibliographie* in 1895. Just like UNISIST, it was a philosophy, a movement, and a program. Although one of the founders, Henri Lafontaine, received the Nobel Prize for Peace in 1913, it failed. In Brussels you can dig today in the archeology of international scientific and technical information. The site is called Mundaneum. Some by-products of the Institute are however still with us: the International Federation for Documentation and the Universal Decimal Classification. I hope that in about ten to twenty years time we shall have the benefit of such important by-products of UNISIST.

UNISIST is viewed in terms of an international movement toward increased voluntary cooperation among the national and the international participating systems and services, using common rules and media, but with varying degrees and modalities of interconnection. When the UNISIST idea was launched about ten years ago, some critics wrote that it was going to be successful because both the United States and Soviet Union wanted it. On the surface this was confirmed by the fact that the UNESCO intergovernmental conference of experts in 1971 adopted UNISIST, and the following General Conference confirmed this adoption; UNISIST became part of UNESCO's 1972–73 program.

UNESCO is such a dream world that I was elected a vice-president of the

UNISIST Intergovernmental Conference at the very moment that I was looking outside the conference hall for an Italian candidate, having been instructed by my government to do so. Later at the General Conference, I voted for UNISIST and its overgrown budget because I did not want to distinguish myself from other delegates. Cooperation with UNESCO is very often a question of conscience.

Such a generalization is never completely true and is even unfair up to a certain point. In my case, it is based upon the intensity of my relation with a division of UNESCO, called DBA, which stands for libraries, documentation, and archives. It would be easy to change my conclusion if it could be related to other divisions of UNESCO, for example, book promotion. Here I had only a sporadic but rewarding experience, centered around International Book Year 1972. But this was, of course, marginal to my main professional interest which I am trying to reflect in the present paper.

The reason why UNISIST was phony from the very beginning is simple indeed. The UNISIST scheme is a fantasy linked to a consumer's society and has nothing to do with the basic problems of developing countries for which UNESCO pretends to stand. When I first voiced this criticism at UNESCO, the answer was: Two of the twenty-two recommendations of the UNISIST program are devoted to developing countries, and those countries request networks for scientific and technical documentation. Let's be serious: First, the two paragraphs are crumbs from a rich table thrown to the poor countries in order to collect their votes; second, UNESCO sends experts to some of those countries, sometimes strange experts, I would say, to draw up government requests for documentation centers or what have you. In the developing country—an expression which does not seem to sound well in the singular—it is organized confusion. Local librarians spend years to develop a public, a university, or a national library, and then suddenly, out of the blue, comes a proposal to build a center or a system or a network—never a simple library—which is a hundred times more expensive. And then comes the confusing sacredness of science in the minds of people and governments which have still to struggle with illiteracy problems. It is a shame for UNESCO to have equated, in too many parts of the world, computers with wisdom, science with happiness.

Before leaving UNISIST I want to tell you an anecdote. One day I was sitting at one of the numerous evaluation committees—on which UNESCO spends too much of its money and of our time—and my neighbor was a French Nobel Prize-winner for Mathematics. He read eloquently a paper written by someone else stating that the whole science community was backing UNISIST. When he had finished and was applauded, I asked him *in aparte*: "Why does the whole science community back UNISIST?" He answered me, "Because we want to mind our own business." I said that this was very respectable indeed and that the librarians also wanted to mind their own business. At this point, I added that cooperation between the two communities has to be worked out. He looked at me very puzzled and said, "But librarians will never be able to distinguish the good papers from the poor ones." I said that this was evident, but I asked if the poor papers were written by librarians? At that moment, someone moved that the responsibility of the research libraries should be transferred from the library division of UNESCO to the science information division!

Universal Bibliographic Control, UBC, is exactly the contrary of UNISIST, when you look at it from its appearance in the UNESCO program. The only clever part about UBC is its acronym. For the rest it has been a shameful courting of UNESCO by IFLA to try to convince the officials that here, with a flexible program which did not require a neologistic jargon, an attempt has been made to improve the daily routine work of libraries all over the world, actually to reduce the routine work and to free the mind for innovative and creative work at all levels in all types of libraries. The aim of UBC could be and actually was summarized in two sentences: a world-wide system for the control and exchange of bibliographical information so as to make universally and promptly available in a form which is internationally acceptable basic bibliographic data on all publications issued in all countries. The concept of Universal Bibliographic Control presupposes the creation of a network made up of component national parts, each of which covers a wide range of publishing and library activities, all integrated at the international level to form a total system.

Such an objective does not require the slightest distinction between industrial countries and developing ones, between capitalistic and socialist states. This is of the utmost importance for efficient international cooperation. The implementation, however, is another story. The simple aim poses quite different problems depending on whether you work with a computer-produced MARC tape of bibliographical descriptions or try to cope with cataloging problems in a country which has not yet been able to produce any kind of a national bibliography. Here a solid and profound cooperation between international governmental and nongovernmental organizations is an absolute must. Let us hope that in the very near future it will effectively be established.

I dwelled for a couple of minutes on the UNESCO share in UNISIST and Universal Bibliographic Control to show that large government resources do not necessarily lead to the best solutions. Nongovernmental organizations, whether national or international, whether in rich or poor countries, are forced by financial pressure to rely on people, on individuals who bring to their work the necessary imagination and who never think of a cumbersome machinery. The real leaders at the international level—for large countries, I could add at the national level too—are those who modify their own ideas when the implementation of their goals runs into red tape. Nothing is more damaging to the life of the mind, in or outside any specific profession, than bureaucracy.

My negative comments on UNISIST have already given me a first opportunity to speak in a positive way about the International Federation for Documentation. Over the years, I have been induced to speak often about FID, from very different angles and more particularly about its cooperation with IFLA. It has been my pleasure to witness and to contribute to closer links between the two organizations. Will there be one day a merger? I hope so, but as one American vice-president of FID put it: Let's work toward this target with due speed. And he was and still is right. Speaking today before an almost exclusively American audience, I may try to compare how the difference between the two organizations changes from the international to the American scene and vice versa. One of the major differences in the organization of IFLA and FID is that the latter has, in each country, a national member, which means that government money is going into the budget of FID. This has a sharper meaning in the United States than in many other countries. At the beginning of this paper

I have already noted that in southern Europe a governmental institutional support replaces the professional organizations. This is certainly not the case with American IFLA members. The result is that a different type of American librarian is active in IFLA and in FID or, at least, that his activity and interest are different in the two organizations. One American librarian once told me: "FID may pretend to be more serious, but IFLA has much more human warmth." He knew both organizations well. I for myself would accept, in this country, a demarcation which I have always refused in the international context: Do the American FID individual members represent science and technology and the American IFLA individual members represent general and public libraries? My answer would be: More in the United States—or for that matter in the Anglo-Saxon world —than anywhere else. The explanation seems rather simple to me. Outside the Anglo-Saxon world and its natural orbit like the Scandinavian countries, the public library movement is underdeveloped, and so most of the librarians from the European continent active in IFLA have come from the national and university libraries. This is much less true regarding the American participants in IFLA activities.

The same observation may also explain why the European antagonism between IFLA and FID has hardly existed in the United States. I can add, between brackets, that it does not explain satisfactorily why Soviet librarians and Soviet documentalists—these are experts in informatics as they like to say—do not speak to one another. A few years ago I was the first link in Moscow between a distinguished senior informaticsian (*sic*) and a no less distinguished senior librarian. They were kind to one another, my interpreter told me, but they had not the slightest interest in one another's work.

I would like to come back for one moment to my oversimplified thesis of science and technology versus public libraries. It is beyond any doubt that this antagonism has weakened during the last generation, also in Europe following in this context the American example. The reasons are manifold and different: active participation of SLA in IFLA, the interest of public libraries in science and technology, the development of public libraries outside the Anglo-Saxon world, for example. If I would try to draw a conclusion from the recent evolution, I would be tempted to say that within FID and within IFLA a growing number of librarians, Americans and non-Americans, are interested in one another's work, but are still aware of differences which mark their daily professional life. And so I endorse the words of the American FID vice-president whom I quoted a few moments ago: Let's strengthen our links with due speed.

To conclude, I would like to use the coincidence between the ALA Centennial and the U.S. Bicentennial to try to generalize from the relationship between the ALA and IFLA to the relationship between the United States and the world. Would it, for example, be appropriate to equate, for this purpose, IRO/ALA with American Studies abroad? This possibility came to my mind when I read Denis Donoghue's comments on a recent Salzburg Seminar on the "Impact of the United States of America and Europe upon Each Other." I quote from Denis Donoghue of Dublin University:

> America Studies: It is clear that this entirely reputable subject has been sustained by many different motives, American foreign policy, the rhetoric of the Cold War, the selfconsciousness of American society, millenarian sentiments rampant in American feeling, and the intrinsic capacity of America to present itself as an object of interest to many people, included gifted scholars. The relation between these several motives is matter for definition and argument. It is not eccentric to find the history and the literature of the United States at least interesting. It is absurd to argue that scholars should turn away from that interest lest they be corrupted by official approval, Washington, the State Department, the American Council of Learned Societies, and the United States Information Service. But there is no merit in assuming that the official relation to American Studies is absolutely pure or disinterested.

The comparison, like most comparisons, is partly true and partly false. What is undoubtedly true is—I should rather say, was—the self-consciousness of American society, the millenarian sentiments, "what is good for us is good for you," and, up to a certain point in time, the official rubber stamp. What is undoubtedly false is that American librarianship as opposed to American Studies never had that kind of "for export only" label. On the contrary, American librarianship found in the world at large an eagerness to be understood, to be adapted to local conditions, to be translated into vernacular situations. This transfer was often very successful because it could be based on an international framework—IFLA—which American librarianship had so powerfully helped to build.

If my last words would give you the impression that, for the purpose of this lecture, I have drawn a dividing line between the United States and the world, which is partly real and partly unreal, it was just to try to explain more easily the flow of ideas which crossed this line.

May I hope that the longstanding working relationship between ALA and IFLA will continue, and even increase, because today, I think it fair to say, American librarianship will be as much an importer as an exporter. It has been an invaluable asset of my professional life, of my life *tout court,* to be a privileged witness of this intellectual migration where the United States has always been a source of inspiration.

Harriet Fleischl Pilpel

Lawyer and senior partner in the firm of Greenbaum, Wolff & Ernst
of New York City

Ms. Pilpel's career has been devoted to issues of civil liberties, freedom of speech and of the press, and problems of the communications media.

She has served on numerous government committees and national boards. She has been Vice-Chairperson of the National Board of Directors of the American Civil Liberties Union and Chairperson of its Communications Media Committee, a member of the Panel of Experts of the U.S. Copyright Office, a trustee of the Copyright Society of the U.S.A., and a member of the Executive Committee of the National Book Committee. She writes frequently on legal issues and intellectual property in *Publishers Weekly*.

With Theodora Zavin, Ms. Pilpel wrote *Rights and Writers* (1960); with Minna Post Peyser, *Know Your Rights* (Women's Bureau, U.S. Department of Labor, 1965); and with Morton David Goldberg, *A Copyright Guide*.

In recognition of her anti-censorship work, Ms. Pilpel was given the annual SIECUS Award (1973) of the Sex Information and Education Council of the United States. For distinguished service in the field of family planning, she received the Margaret Sanger Award (1974) of the Planned Parenthood Federation of America.

LIBRARIES AND THE FIRST AMENDMENT

I WANT TO ADMIT at the outset of this talk a tremendous prejudice in favor of libraries based on early personal experience with them. When I was a small child, the biggest event every week in our lives (actually it was every two weeks because we always kept the books two weeks) was my mother's taking my sister and me to the library. We were allowed to take only two books out of that library, one fiction and one nonfiction. Therefore I especially enjoy my experience as a grandmother today, for every week or every two weeks I take my grandchildren to the library where we are allowed to take out six books and no distinction is made between fiction and nonfiction.

I had a particularly interesting examination in ancient history during my freshman year at Vassar. I boned up on the historical events and people but when we came to the exam room, the professor handed each of us a slip of paper on which were a few words—a different few words for each student. Mine were "Athene-Minerva." Our professor said, "This is not an examination to test your knowledge because I really don't care how much you have learned. I want to know how good you are at finding out." We were given three hours to go to the library and get together a bibliography and any substance we might pick up along the way. I learned a lot about where to find material about Athene-Minerva, and I never forgot that exam. In many ways it was the only exam I ever took that made sense. The proof of the pudding was that when I applied to Columbia Law School the dean looked at my record and he said: "You come from Vassar; we're happy to have Vassar girls here; they don't know much but there is nothing they can't find out."

I am very grateful, therefore, to libraries and librarians. I think that you

87

exemplify the science of finding out, and I am deeply flattered and very thrilled to be here with you today.

I thought I would look up some definitions with which to start my talk today but none of the ones I found seemed to be right. For example, I looked up the word "censor," and the source said: "one of two magistrates of Rome who took a register of the number and property of citizens, administered the public finances and exercised the office of morals and conduct." The definition just didn't seem to fit what I wanted to talk about. I am going to skip the definitions, therefore, and turn at once to the First Amendment.

The First Amendment provides that the government shall make no law abridging freedom of speech or of the press. I guess that I should at least try to define what I mean by "law." One definition is Dickens's—"the law is a ass"—and indeed it is quite often. It also can be defined, however, in a variety of other ways. We should bear in mind that we have at least four sources of law in this country, and I am sure you all come in contact with all of them at one time or another. First, we have the Federal Constitution, which contains the First Amendment, and the state Constitutions, most or all of which contain similar clauses about freedom of the press. Then we have federal law made by Congress which generally governs interstate and foreign commerce and the mails. State law made by the state legislatures usually applies to what goes on within a state. However, legislation is by no means the only source of law. Law is also derived from the decisions and opinions of judges, the rulings of administrative agencies, and common practice or usage.

We should bear in mind, also, the distinction between criminal and civil law; for example, obscenity is typically a criminal offense, whereas privacy laws and libel laws are ordinarily the subject of civil suits.

I have at hand also a definition of a lawyer which I am going to read because so many unpleasant definitions of members of the bar are popular today. "An attorney is an explorer, always going into new territory." I do hope that you will remember that the next time someone says "the law is a ass."

I am particularly pleased to be a speaker at your centennial celebration.

I looked back a hundred years and found, as you all know, that the first public library was in Peterboro, New Hampshire, in 1833 and that this organization of librarians came into being in 1876. I was reminded that three years before the founding of the ALA there had been a severe business panic (I wondered if there was any connection but I doubt it). At that time, according to Gore Vidal's book *1876*, the United States already had more prosperous magazines and newspapers than all of Europe put together. However, we had little social consciousness and children were permitted to starve and freeze in the streets during the panic of 1873. The forces of censorship were, of course, not concerned with the starvation and dying of children but with what seemed to them the salacious appeal of Flaubert's *Madame Bovary* and of "an American poet" described in a book I read as "much disliked by the prudish American reviewers, a man named Walt Whitman who lives in Camden, New Jersey." At the same time that some of today's classics were thus frowned upon, there was in fact a certain amount of, shall we say, dilly-dallying going on. It was reported for example, that Henry Ward Beecher was giving his sermons every Sunday in the presence of twenty former mistresses.

We were in 1876 still aware of the recent end of the Civil War. There was a lot of talk about how the nation's Centennial would bind up the nation's wounds—the wounds were surely deeper then than now but I do think the Bicentennial is serving the same function. In 1876 the kinds of little gimmicks that were sold were, for example, moustache cups, lard cans, and hand fans. Much as I looked in the city of New York on the day of the tall ships, I found none of those.

In my reading preparation for today, I also found that in 1908, as I am sure you know, Arthur Bostwick of the New York Public Library, became president of the ALA. He chose as the subject for his inaugural address "The Librarian as Censor." At that time being a censor was an approved role and not a criticism as it is today. An article in the *Library Journal* of June 1, 1975, reports that "in the 1890's the highest function of the librarian was to exercise the subtle discernment that would distinguish innocent from vicious amusement." In 1895 Theresa West of the Milwaukee Public Library in a symposium dealing with "improper books" and how to exclude them, said that the policy for a library "which is essentially for the people is that books which speak with truth about normal, wholesome conditions may be safely bought however plain spoken; while on the other hand, books which treat of morbid diseased conditions of the individual man or of society are intended for the student of special subjects."

It is interesting that eighty-odd years ago there was such a totally different concept of the function of the librarian. Today, of course, librarians and ALA are the leaders in all anti-censorship battles. I have never been in an anti-censorship battle, and I have engaged in many, in which ALA was not at the forefront with its Intellectual Freedom Committee and with the dedicated efforts of such people as Bob Wedgeworth, Judy Krug, Alex Allain, and many, many others.

Before reviewing the specifics of the censorship struggle today, let us consider a description of today's world, in which the censorship battle goes on. It comes from an unlikely source, namely the *London Rotarian*. It says:

> Let us look at the world as if it were a village with a population of 1,000. In this village there would be 150 North and South Americans, sixty of them representing the United States, 210 Europeans, 36 Africans, 565 Asians. There would be 300 white people and 700 non-white people. Of the 1,000 people, 300 would be Christians, half the total income of the village would be in the United States. Almost all the affluent part of the village would be composed of Christians from Europe and North America, over 700 of the 1,000 villagers would be unable to read, over 500 would be suffering from malnutrition, over 800 would live in substandard housing, not more than ten would have a university education.

We all know that in the world today there is an enormous need for libraries and librarians. I cite the Rockford, Illinois, Public Library not because it is different from other public libraries, but because I gather it is fairly typical of what libraries can do and are doing. It seems to me to do absolutely everything: They distribute books, magazines, paintings, sculptures, records, slides, films and film strips, on all subjects. They have special service to nursing homes and shut-ins; they are information centers for everyday as well as for reference problems; they have classes for adults and children, and they even have degree-giving programs. Clearly, libraries have marched very distinctly forward since the days when we were allowed one fiction and one nonfiction book.

Now, let's look at the censorship pattern today. Much to my astonishment I found that most of the instances of censorship I came across fell conveniently under the letters "RSVP." Each seemed to belong under one of the following headings: R—*religion* and race; S—*sex*; V—*violence*; and P—*politics*. I will take a brief look at today's pattern of censorship under these headings.

In the old days, censorship on grounds related to religion was widespread and appeared under the headings of sacrilege, heresy, blasphemy, and so on. Witches were sometimes burned at the stake when guilty of these. Today there is much less religious censorship but the memory lingers on, and there are hints of it in some of our best-known recent censorship cases. You are all, I'm sure, familiar with the famous case of *Near* v. *Minnesota* decided in 1931 in which the Supreme Court held that publication could not, consistent with the Constitution, be enjoined in advance. The government can punish abuses of the press after they occur, but it may not suppress in advance; that is, it may not impose what is known technically as a "prior restraint." The Near case involved a series of newspaper stories stating that Jewish gangsters controlled gambling and bootlegging in Minneapolis. This series was the subject of an injunction (issued by a lower court) which the Supreme Court held was unconstitutional. The series said, for example, that "practically every vendor of vile hootch . . . every snake-faced gangster and embryonic yegg in the Twin Cities is a Jew. It is Jew, Jew, Jew as long as one cares to comb over the records." Chief Justice Hughes speaking for the United States Supreme Court said that "the fact that for 150 years there has been almost an entire absence of attempts to impose previous restraints upon publication is significant of the deep sense of conviction that such restrains would violate Constitutional rights," as indeed they do.

More recently in the Kanawha County dispute in West Virginia, Judge Hall said that although the books there involved were accused of being obscene and "un-Christian," they nonetheless could not be banned. Recently, too, I found out that the Joint Committee on Printing in Washington refused to print in the *Congressional Record* a pro-censorship Congressman's remarks about the books involved in the Island Trees School Board controversy on Long Island. The ground of the refusal was that "the general rules governing the Record [the *Congressional Record*] prohibit inclusion therein of profanity, obscene wording or vulgarisms." So they refused to print the relevant excerpts from works of Bernard Malamud, Oliver LaFarge, Desmond Morris, Piri Thomas, Richard Wright, Langston Hughes, and Kurt Vonnegut. It is interesting to note that Wayne Hayes was chairman of this joint committee, and it was he who said that the committee had an "ancient rule" that "profanity, obscenity or extreme vulgarisms" must be replaced at the printers with "asterisks and dashes."

Racist slurs are sometimes the basis of censorship and some groups would try to prevent such slurs by law. I disagree for reasons I will discuss later on. It is not exactly race censorship we worry about today; it is coping with racist literature, which I will also cover later.

So we come to censorship as to sex—words or described deeds, both being often identified by "asterisks and dashes." I first want to point out that the Supreme Court itself has held that sex and obscenity are not synonymous, which I find very reassuring:

> . . . sex and obscenity are not synonymous. Obscene material is material which deals with sex in a manner appealing to prurient interest. The portrayal of sex, e.g., in art, literature and scientific works, is not itself sufficient reason to deny material the constitutional protection of freedom of speech and press. Sex, a great and mysterious motive force in human life, has indisputably been a subject of absorbing interest to mankind through the ages; it is one of the vital problems of human interest and public concern.

I will divide my discussion of sex censorship into the two categories I just mentioned, specific words on the one hand and depicted actions on the other. I have found that the word which I will spell "f-u-c-k" seems to create the greatest single problem—much more, for example, than the word "s-h-i-t." The use of f-u-c-k in a motion picture, at least until very recently, automatically called for an R (Restricted) classification, which means kids cannot go to see the picture except with an adult; the use of the word s-h-i-t did not and does not call for this classification. It can, for example, be a PG (Parental Guidance Suggested) movie. I found all this out because of what happened with reference to the film "All the President's Men." That superb film was originally classified as an R picture. Having read the book and knowing the subject matter, I could think of no reason for this. When I asked why, I was told it was because characters used the word f-u-c-k.

Several of us who disagreed with the R classification for this picture got in touch with the film rating board of the Motion Picture Association of America. Warner Brothers, whose picture it was, presented several special private previews of the picture to selected audiences of community leaders in New York City. I remember at the one preview that I attended, walking out with someone who asked me why f-u-c-k made a movie an R while s-h-i-t did not. None of us could figure it out, and happily the appeals board reversed the earlier classification and reclassified "All the President's Men" as PG.

I had a conversation recently with my 11-year-old granddaughter which is pertinent. I asked her if she wanted to see a certain movie, and she said, "No, of course not." She was so positive that I asked, "Why, have you heard it's no good?" She replied, "No, I didn't hear it was no good, but I know it is a G [for General Audiences] picture." She went on to say that she didn't like G pictures because "they're mostly not interesting and about animals." She added that generally she and her friends preferred PG pictures.

The reason why I dare even discuss the use of the word "f-u-c-k" is that there was a memorable case in the United States Supreme Court which involved that word. A young man went into a courthouse with a sweat-shirt on the back of which appeared "fuck the draft." He was arrested and charged and convicted of a criminal offense. The case went all the way to the United States Supreme Court. Justice Harlan, who was not known as a flaming radical, held that the words on the shirt were a legitimate expression of the man's opinion about the draft and the Viet Nam War. The conviction was reversed, and in a very real sense the taboo word acquired some constitutional protection.

I have had other experiences with that and other so-called dirty words like it. Some time ago in California there was a great deal of agitation about the *Dictionary of American Slang,* which was on the shelves of many libraries. The dictionary was attacked because it included many dirty words. As part of their campaign against the book, its opponents collected all the dirty words and put them together in a small publication to show why the *Dictionary of American Slang* should not be allowed in the libraries. Actually, of course, the collection in one place of all the dirty words was very popular—and no doubt many people saw it who would not in the normal course have come into contact with the dictionary itself.

I will now turn to the kind of sex censorship that deals with the description of sex acts. I want to start with a quote from the United States Supreme Court recent decisions: " 'Obscenities' means those slang words currently generally rejected for regular use in mixed society, that are used to refer to genitals, female breasts, sexual conduct or excretory functions or products, either that have no other meaning or that in context are clearly used for their bodily, sexual or excretory meaning." I remember when Edmund Wilson's story of the Princess with the Golden Hair was censored. It was part of his *Memoirs of Hecate County.* It was censored in New York State, I believe because it suggested that women had orgasms, a subject which apparently had not been discussed in respectable print before. Although, however, *Hecate County* was censored in New York, it was not held to be obscene in New Jersey. On a few occasions when I was coming back from William Dix's Princeton, there were actually vendors on the road to the Hudson tunnel, saying, "Buy a copy of *Hecate County* here. You can't get it once you cross the line to New York." Again I suspect the attack served only to stir up additional interest in the book.

About that time I had a rather nightmarish censorship experience in Washington in connection with a book entitled *Nightmare Alley*. The book had not been charged with obscenity while it was in hard cover, but it was challenged as obscene by the United States Post Office Department when it went into paperback. I am sure you all realize that happens often. Apparently it is thought that those who can afford hard cover prices are incorruptible but not so those who buy paperbacks. I went to Washington to try to persuade the Post Office Department that *Nightmare Alley* could not be adjudged obscene. We went through it page by page. One of the staff had underlined all "objectionable" words. Although most of them did not seem objectionable to me, I could understand that others might find some of them so. In the course of reviewing the book, I came across some underlinings which seemed absurd to me and which prompted me to say, "How far can you go with this insanity? Here is a simple allusion to fruit and you have underlined it." The simple allusion to fruit was a statement to the effect that one of the characters in the book had "left a trail of busted cherries" behind him. When I said this, the two Post Office lawyers looked at each other, excused themselves hastily and went into the next room. Eventually they came back and with some embarrassment said, "Those underlined words were not a 'simple allusion to fruit' but meant 'ruptured maidenheads.' " I apologized for my stupidity in not knowing that and pointed out that if I didn't understand it, I didn't think most readers would, and, furthermore, that those who did understand it must know all about it already, so how could it hurt them?

I went back to New York with a long list of these and other words and expressions to which they had objected, but shortly after they decided to let *Nightmare Alley* go through. I think they were not particularly anxious to pursue the matter further and risk having to "educate" me again.

I find great confusion as to the basis of sex censorship. For example, many people who see nothing wrong with having freely available in their homes *Playboy, Fear of Flying*, or the *National Geographic* (with its pictures of naked natives in various parts of the world) get very excited when schools and libraries want to make available books on sex and reproduction. My own experience with my own children was interesting. I worked on many cases involving what the prosecution considered dirty books. With one exception I did not attempt to hide them from my children. The one exception was *Tropic of Cancer,* which I hid in my bureau drawer, not because I thought it obscene but because I thought it might turn young people off of sex rather than on to sex. However, I needn't have worried. One day another little boy came to visit my son. I had not deliberately let *Lady Chatterley's Lover* lie on the table in the living room but it was indeed there. The visiting little boy asked, "What is that book?" My son replied, "That's one of those stupid things my mother has to work on." I don't believe my children ever looked at any of the books I brought home; they just assumed they were boring.

Lately the Supreme Court decisions have cut down on freedom of the press, but perhaps their recent restrictive decisions have not worked out as badly as many of us feared they would. In Oklahoma City in 1973, the district attorney stated that as far as he was concerned the only books that were completely safe under the recent United States Supreme Court opinions were *Rebecca of Sunnybrook Farm* and *Black Beauty.* Yet at that time, as you may recall, the best-selling work of fiction was *Once Is Not Enough* by Jacqueline Susann and the best-selling work of nonfiction was *The Joy of Sex* by Alex Comfort, both of them a far cry from *Rebecca of Sunnybrook Farm* and *Black Beauty.*

We are certainly better off as far as sex censorship is concerned than we were a hundred years ago. An historian friend of mine told me that years ago there used to be "ladies' days" at museums. It was considered improper for men to be around when ladies looked at, for example, nude statues. Even on "ladies' day" some museums frequently put covers over some of the paintings. When I asked, "Why over the paintings and not over the sculpture?," I was told that the flesh colors, etc., on nude figures might be more than ladies could bear. In fact, we have advanced very far since those days. Jutting out in front of the Whitney Museum on Madison Avenue in New York, there has been for some time a very large figure of a naked woman. I mentioned to this same friend that I was surprised that no one had objected to its being there. He pointed out that because her hands were chained together, she was obviously a captive and couldn't help herself and that made it all right, he said.

I'm sure I don't have to remind this audience of the Commission on Obscenity and Pornography which found that in any event there is absolutely no reliable evidence to indicate that exposure to explicit sexual materials plays any role in the causation of delinquent or criminal sexual behavior among youths or adults.

Since the most recent group of obscenity cases was decided a couple of years ago, twenty-three states have passed new obscenity laws. Six of these, I'm told by Judy Krug and her staff, are really protective of the First Amendment. Just a few weeks ago the United States Supreme Court sustained a measure which has unfortunate censorship aspects. In a case involving Detroit zoning regulations, the Court, through Judge Stevens who wrote the majority opinion, said in effect that all speech is free but some speech is freer than other speech:

> There is surely a less vital interest in the uninhibited exhibition of material that is on the borderline between pornography and artistic expression than in the free dissemination of ideas of social and political significance. [*Young* v. *American Mini Theatres Inc.,* June 24, 1976]

He added:

> Few of us would march our sons and daughters off to war to press the citizens' right to see specific sexual activities exhibited in the theatre of our choice.

In a dissent in another earlier case promulgating relatively restrictive standards for determining obscenity, Justice Douglas had said:

> If the decision of the Court is to be taken literally [on sex], the American library system as we know it will be destroyed. It takes but a short while to purge a library collection. Hitler accomplished it in one night.

Sex is by far the most usual basis for censorship, although today there is a rising tide of objection to the depictions of violence which abound on our television screens. Many years ago I was defending in court a book entitled *The Gilded Hearse*. The New York Society for the Suppression of Vice, which had at the time prosecutorial powers, had attacked the book as obscene. I think the attack came because the book contained a description of a scene in a lower berth in which a man and woman, not married to each other, had sexual relations. I never knew whether the objection was made because the copulation might have been in interstate commerce or what. Mr. Sumner, an official of the Society for the Suppression of Vice, personally did the prosecuting. I called as a witness in favor of the book and its author Dr. Frederick Wertham, who was and is very well known for his opposition to graphically depicted violence. He had carried into court with him a rather shabby brown paper parcel tied up with string. He is a most impressive-looking man and somehow the parcel did not fit well with the rest of him. I suggested that he check it, which he refused to do. When I called him as a witness, he brought the brown paper parcel with him to the witness stand. I tried to ignore the parcel and proceeded to ask him if he thought there was anything in the book which was obscene and he said unequivocally that there was not. In the course of his cross examination Mr. Sumner asked Dr. Wertham whether indeed he thought anything was obscene. Dr. Wertham's eyes lit up. Out came the brown paper parcel, the contents of which turned out to be so-called comic books abounding with violent scenes. (One, I remember, showed a man gouging out a woman's eye with a hypodermic needle.) Dr. Wertham testified at some length as to his opinion that this was the kind of material that could really "corrupt," and he spread the "comic books" all over the witness box. I think Mr. Sumner must have regretted that he had asked the question which brought on such a torrent of information about the evil effects of the depiction of violence as opposed to sex. The case was dismissed—*The Gilded Hearse* continued to circulate.

As you no doubt all know, Chicago has a new ordinance which attempts to define harmful violence and to prevent children under 18 years from viewing excessively violent films. I don't know enough about this to be authoritative, but it seems to me that this is a form of censorship which will probably not accomplish its purpose. Perhaps a better way of reaching the same goal is reflected in a recent article in the *New York Times*. It was headed, "Does Violence Sell?" and it reported a survey which showed that 10 percent of a sample of adult viewers had considered not buying a product because it had been advertised on excessively violent programs and 8 percent had said they actually had not bought the product for that reason. I would not oppose that approach and I think it might work.

The final initial of RSVP censorship is *P* which stands for politics. There is not as much censorship today on political grounds as there used to be. A recent study of Philadelphia area libraries showed that books which challenge conventional sexual mores meet with more caution, anxiety, and defensiveness than books that challenge prevalent political values and practices. "Thus *Soul on Ice*, Guevara's Diary and the *Autobiography of Malcolm X* will make their way more readily into our collections," said the study, "than *Tropic of Cancer* or *Our Lady of the Flowers*."

I want to make clear at this point that in criticizing censorship in the United States, I do not overlook the fact that compared with much of the rest of the world, we have a very free-press society indeed. In Brazil, for example, in April a televised program of the Bolshoi Ballet, which was beamed to 110 other countries, was not allowed to be aired, apparently because it might induce a favorable view of the Soviet Union. Nor can it any longer be said that India is "a middle way." There, according to a recent report, "the censorship is within us now—we often don't need the censor to tell us what not to do—it has gotten to be automatic."

What I am saying, however, is that we have more censorship, primarily on "RSVP" grounds, than we should have. Last month, for example, the West Orange, New Jersey, Policemen's Benevolent Association objected to Eve Merriam's *Inner City Mother Goose* because it was, in their opinion, anti-police. That's not, of course, as egregious an example of political censorship as the one some years ago when a woman member of an Indiana textbook group demanded that stories about Robin Hood be removed from the schools. In her opinion, Robin Hood's habit of stealing from the rich and giving to the poor was "the Communist line. It's just a smearing of law and order and everything that disrupts law and order is their meat." Someone thought of writing to the then Sheriff of Nottingham about this, and I understand he answered that whatever else Robin Hood may have been, he was not a Communist.

In Mel Brooks' TV series about a sort of Robin Hood, when the question arose whether Robin stole from the rich and gave to the poor, the answer was, "Certainly not—Robin steals from the rich and he steals from the poor and keeps everything."

There are other areas of censorship not directly related to my RSVPs—religion, race, sex, politics, and violence. The right of privacy, for example, has been used to suppress books and has been the basis of court decisions which, in my opinion, constitute a real threat to freedom of expression. In a recent case, for example, a reporter visited the wife of a man who had perished when a bridge had collapsed. The visit was six months after the event and the lower court found that the story contained some inaccuracies. The writer and the publication in which the article appeared were sued by the widow for violation of her "right of privacy." Her claim was upheld by the United States Supreme Court, which found that the story contained misstatements although it was not libelous. If our law is going to take the position that a court can judge what is true and what is false, and base damage judgments on the ground of nonlibelous falsehoods, we are facing a very real censorship threat on privacy grounds. Justice Douglas, dissenting in the case, said:

> The press will be "free" in the First Amendment sense when the judge-made qualifications of that freedom are withdrawn and the substance of the First Amendment restored to what I believe was the purpose of its enactment.

Recent libel cases also are restricting freedom of expression. The present Supreme Court in the *Firestone* v. *Time Magazine* case held that although certainly many members of the public are interested in the sexual activities of high-society people, they were not the kind of public interest figures which called for a strict libel rule. The court sustained the libel judgment against Time, Incorporated, for printing statements about the case which, in effect, had already appeared in newspapers all over the country.

There are also contempt of court laws, laws against nuisances, zoning laws such as the Detroit law I mentioned before—all these forms of covert censorship represent the kind of thing which ALA in general and all of you individually should and will watch. These, too, can narrow the choice of books you have for your library.

I have always, I thought, been steadfast in my devotion to the First Amendment. However, I suddenly realized that I, too, might in some respects be somewhat censorship minded, and so might many of my anti-censorship friends. I, for example, do not like it when I see Mr. Dickens' stereotype of an atrocious Jew in the person of Fagin and Mr. Shakespeare's in the person of Shylock. I have heard recently of people who think Huckleberry Finn should not be allowed in libraries because of the constant references to "Nigger" Jim. The whole question as to what to do with racial and religious stereotypes is a difficult one, and I certainly cannot solve it for myself, much less for anyone else. On balance, however, I'm convinced that censorship is not the answer in any event.

I do approve of studies exposing racial and sex stereotypes such as the study done recently in Kalamazoo which exposed sexist stereotypes. I'm pretty sure, moreover, that all of you would agree with me that the fact that a book is racist or sexist does not mean that it should be removed from libraries even though you yourself are very much against sexism and racism. The answer, I guess, is to be sufficiently sensitized to such material that you know what it is and can expose it for what it is to others.

In the final analysis I always come back to the great "anti-censorship thinkers." Voltaire's "I disapprove of what you say but I will defend to the death your right to say it"; John Milton's "Give me the liberty to utter and to argue freely according to conscience above all liberties. . . . Let [Truth] and Falsehood grapple; who ever knew Truth put to the worse in a free and open encounter?" Justice Cardozo, I believe, correctly described freedom of speech and of the press as "the matrix, the indispensable condition, of nearly every other form of freedom." And Justice Harlan summed it all up most succinctly when he said, "The constitutional right of free expression 'is powerful medicine in a society as diverse and populous as ours.'"

What I finally came to in pondering the question of libraries and the First Amendment was what I call "neutral principles." I am not sure that is precisely the right phrase for them, but it is my shorthand way of saying that all ideas and depictions should be welcome in a free marketplace of thought. In a way, that's the kind of marketplace the Fairness Doctrine aims at accomplishing in connection with radio and television. The situation, of course, is quite different for the print media. It is different because in connection with the electronic media there is a technological scarcity and the station licensees, in effect, enjoy a government monopoly.

It is the principles behind the Fairness Doctrine that seem to me neutral principles which should be a guide to all those who to a greater or lesser extent determine what the rest of us will see, hear, and read. I have in mind such guideposts as the need to present many sides of public issues; the right of individuals who are personally attacked to reply, and so forth. I am not suggesting that the Fairness Doctrine should apply to the print media. I am simply saying that the principles behind it which have been sustained by the United States Supreme Court are among the neutral principles which I hope will govern our marketplace of thought. I would hope that we would not tolerate anyone's being prosecuted or any book's being removed from a library on the ground of disagreement with its content. An example of a content neutral approach can be seen in two recent filmstrips. The winner of the best Bicentennial filmstrip of the year for 1976 was a strip called "The American Revolution—Who Was Right?" When I went to school that question would have been unthinkable—as well as unaskable. It would have seemed incredible to most of us then that there were two sides to the American Revolution. In any event, for kids today it is a very good idea to have something called "The American Revolution—Who Was Right?" with the same visual being used for two different audios, one discussing the question from the English point of view and the other giving the American side. A similar presentation is to be found in a filmstrip entitled "Great Trials, Pro and Con," with one audio presenting the arguments of the prosecution and the other the arguments of the defense—again with one visual.

So, where do I really end up? I mutter to myself from time to time, "Seek not for whom the bell tolls." Some of the more recent content-oriented decisions of the United States Supreme Court on obscenity, of course, could have and may still have an unfortunate impact directly on libraries. Justice Douglas in one of those cases three years ago said:

> What we do today is rather ominous as respects librarians. The net now designed by the Court is so finely meshed that taken literally it could result in raids on libraries. Libraries, I had always assumed, were sacrosanct, representing every part of the spectrum. If what is offensive to the most influential person or group in a community can be purged from a library, the library system would be destroyed.

> A few States exempt librarians from laws curbing distribution of "obscene" literature. California's law, however, provides: "Every person, who with knowledge that a person is a minor, or who fails to exercise reasonable care in ascertaining the true age of a minor, knowingly distributes to or sends or causes to be sent to, or exhibits to, or offers to distribute or exhibit any harmful matter to a minor is guilty of a misdemeanor." [9 Ann. Calif. Code 313.1.]

The fact that our libraries have not been destroyed or, for the most part, substantially adversely affected by content-oriented censorship is due in no small part to ALA, which is always in a lead position in the anti-censorship battle.

There is another problem for libraries. Librarians as civil servants often find themselves in the delicate position of being—I am quoting now by the way from a librarian—"the guardians of much that is necessarily controversial while they are placed low on the totem pole of authority—given very little power to defend their professional opinions and their personal security." As I mentioned before in connection with the global village in which 700 people out of 1000 could not read, "The world still has to learn to read if mind-art (words) is to be as important as see-art or hear-art. Literature is a poor cousin today. . . ." Moreover "those with funds to support literature should try hard to support the risky and the vital not just what is safely past (few people kill each other any more about attitudes concerning Alexander Hamilton)."

The ALA *Intellectual Freedom Manual* makes clear that librarians have responded to the censorship challenge and have risen to it. I am not going to quote much of this to you since you all know it, but I found some of it so exciting that I would like your permission to quote and to agree with both of the following statements:

> Libraries should provide books and other materials presenting all points of view concerning the problems and issues of our times; no library materials should be proscribed or removed from libraries because of partisan or doctrinal disapproval.

That is, the criteria should be content neutral, and no book should be censored on RSVP grounds: religion or race, sex, violence or politics, or indeed on any content-oriented ground. Perhaps we will detest Nazism and all it stands for even more if we have had the opportunity to read Adolph Hitler's *Mein Kampf*.

The other statement I want to quote is from your "Intellectual Freedom Statement":

> We will make available to everyone who needs or desires them the widest possible diversity of views and modes of expression, including those which are strange, unorthodox or unpopular. . . . Only through continuous weighing and selection from among opposing views can free individuals obtain the strength needed for intelligent, constructive decisions and actions. In short, we need to understand not only what we believe, but why we believe as we do.

In concluding, I want to say that while I don't think Morris Ernst or I can claim credit for the library postage rates, we did play an important part in getting the first special book-postage rate established. President Roosevelt said he was happy to decree a special low postage rate for books in this country while Hitler and his cohorts were burning books abroad.

Today, when others are witch-hunting books, ALA is holding high the banners of Voltaire, Milton, et al. The American Library Association has been in the forefront fighting for freedom of expression along with such other organizations as the Association of American Publishers, the American Civil Liberties Union, the Authors League of America, and many others—frequently inspired by ALA leadership.

On this centennial occasion, you, the American Library Association, have much to be proud of. I am deeply grateful to you for letting me share this happy time with you.

ADDENDUM

Since I delivered the foregoing speech on July 23, 1976, the United States Court of Appeals for the Sixth Circuit has handed down a very important decision in the case of *Minarcini* v. *Strongsville City School District and Bingham*. The case involved the selection of books for use as high school texts and for inclusion in high school libraries. Since much of what the Court said in its opinion is highly relevant to any discussion of "libraries and the First Amendment," I thought it would be a good idea to add the following self-explanatory excerpts from the Strongsville decision:

> Clearly, discretion as to the selection of textbooks must be lodged somewhere and we can find no federal constitutional prohibition which prevents its being lodged in school board officials who are elected representatives of the people. . . . On the other hand, "[t]he vigilant protection of constitutional freedoms is nowhere more vital than in the community of American schools, . . .

> [Quoting from the United States Supreme Court] As this Court said . . . the First Amendment "does not tolerate laws that cast a pall of orthodoxy over the classroom."

> A library is a storehouse of knowledge. When created for a public school it is an important privilege created by the state for the benefit of the students in the school. That privilege is not subject to being withdrawn by succeeding school boards whose members might desire to "winnow" the library for books the content of

which occasioned their displeasure or disapproval. Of course, a copy of a book may wear out. Some books may become obsolete. Shelf space alone may at some point require some selection of books to be retained and books to be disposed of. No such rationale is involved in this case, however. . . ."

. . . we must conclude that the School Board removed the books because it found them objectionable in content and because it felt that it had the power, unfettered by the First Amendment, to censor the school library for subject matter which the Board members found distasteful.

Neither the State of Ohio nor the Strongsville School Board was under any federal constitutional compulsion to provide a library for the Strongsville High School or to choose any particular books. Once having created such a privilege for the benefit of its students, however, neither body could place conditions on the use of the library which were related solely to the social or political tastes of school board members. . . .

The removal of books from a school library is a much more serious burden upon freedom of classroom discussion than . . . [other] action found unconstitutional. . . .

The Library is a mighty resource in the free marketplace of ideas . . . It is specially dedicated to broad dissemination of ideas. It is a forum for silent speech.

. . . We believe that the language . . . , plus the recent cases . . . serve to establish firmly both the First Amendment right to know which is involved in our instant case and the standing of the student plaintiff to raise the issue.

The Court's decision was "to direct the members of the Strongsville School Board to replace in the library the books with which these resolutions dealt, by purchase, if necessary, out of the first sums available for library purposes."

Daniel J. Boorstin

Twelfth Librarian of Congress, author, historian, and educator

---

From 1944 to 1969 Mr. Boorstin was a member of the faculty of the University of Chicago. Leaving that University as Preston and Sterling Morton Distinguished Service Professor of History, he became in 1969 Director of the National Museum of History and Technology of the Smithsonian Institution. Four years later he relinquished his duties as Director to become Senior Historian. He was sworn in as Librarian of Congress on November 12, 1975.

His many publications include a three-part work: *The Americans—The Colonial Experience* (1958, Bancroft Prize), *The National Experience* (1965, Parkman Prize), and *The Democratic Experience* (1973, Pulitzer and Dexter prizes). Other books include *The Lost World of Thomas Jefferson* (1948), *The Image* (1962), and *Democracy and Its Discontents* (1974). Mr. Boorstin has served on various public commissions, including the American Revolution Bicentennial Commission and the State Department Indo-American Subcommission on Education and Cultural Affairs.

He is a trustee of Colonial Williamsburg in Virginia.

INTRODUCTION OF DANIEL J. BOORSTIN

Keyes D. Metcalf

This being our one hundredth anniversary, your chairman and I agreed that instead of simply introducing the afternoon speaker, I should talk also briefly about his four predecessors as Librarian of Congress, each of whom I have known and worked with closely.

Herbert Putnam, the first of the four, was appointed in 1899 but I met him first in 1911. He continued in office for forty years, until 1939 when he was 78. From the prospective of my 87 years, it appears to me that this was a mistake.

In 1931 I became chairman of the ALA Cooperative Cataloguing Committee, and during the next six years I spent about one hundred days at the Library of Congress, always making a courtesy call on Mr. Putnam and often having lunch with him or going with him on his daily walk through the library, during which he talked over his library problems in detail. He was *the* great librarian of his day but a younger man might have accomplished more during the last years.

I became acquainted with Mr. Putnam's successor, Archibald MacLeish, when he came to Harvard in 1938 as curator of the Neiman Fellows. Early in the spring of 1939 Archie told me in confidence that President Roosevelt wanted to nominate him as the next Librarian of Congress. He asked me what the librarian had to do. In the light of my experience with Mr. Putnam, I told him what I thought, and Archie said frankly, "This is not what I want to do. I would much prefer to spend my time in writing." We had four more talks during the spring, always with the same conclusion.

At the ALA Conference in 1939, just after Mr. MacLeish had been nominated, some extremely regrettable remarks were made about him. In spite of this unfortunate beginning, Archie called for help from a first-class group of librarians (including Quincy Mumford) and the resulting much needed reorganization carried out by MacLeish was remarkably successful; I doubt that any trained librarian could have done as well so quickly.

After five years Archie became Assistant Secretary of State. Some of us—who knew that the President would not nominate a trained librarian—went to him without ALA authorization and suggested to him the dean of one of our great University Graduate Schools. FDR agreed to nominate him but his death intervened, and incoming President Truman appointed the Associate Librarian, Luther Evans, who was not a trained librarian. The fact that Luther had been born west of the Mississippi may have been in his favor with Truman. In any case, because of his untiring efforts on our behalf, Luther became more popular with librarians than any other Librarian of Congress had ever been. I had the pleasure of working closely with him on two important Library of Congress committees. Luther was not as successful with the Congress as he was with librarians, and he was glad to resign to become head of UNESCO.

I was chairman of the ALA committee to wait on President Eisenhower with suggestions for Luther's successor. We submitted a list of half a dozen names including that of L. Quincy Mumford. I have been told that Mumford was selected because he came from North Carolina and no one knew whether he was a Republican or a Democrat. Too few of us will remember that while Quincy may not have managed his relations with all librarians as well as his untrained predecessors, he presided over many great achievements that are changing our whole library picture. The annual budget of the Library of Congress was increased from $9,000,000 to $100,000,000. The Madison Building, which is now quite well on its way to completion, was authorized. The MARC cataloging project, which is rapidly helping to solve what for many of us has been our most difficult problem, was established, and on a second attempt the Cataloging in Publication is flourishing, and the Union List of Serials for Canada and the United States is well on its way.

With this as background, I finally come to my primary assignment—the introduction of the new Librarian of Congress to his first American Library Association Conference. I will be brief.

All of you must have known Dr. Boorstin as one of our most popular American historians. This reminds me of the fact that my three predecessors and my successor at Harvard were historians—including Justin Winsor, the first president of the American Library Association just one hundred years ago.

Let me point out also that Mr. Putnam and Mr. MacLeish were law school graduates and that Luther Evans became a successful law librarian at Columbia. Dr. Boorstin pursued legal studies and received degrees at Oxford and the Inner Temple in London and is both a historian, as were four Harvard librarians, and involved in the law as three great Librarians of Congress have been in this century.

I will now venture impolitely to give our speaker some advice. You are in a position in which you cannot catch up even if you work sixty hours a week. You will need all the help you can get from your fine staff and from the library profession at large, and you will have no trouble in obtaining this help. Finally, do not try to follow my example and stay in library work for more than seventy years.

In spite of my age, I try to keep in close touch with the library world, and from all I can learn you have made a remarkably good start during the past eight months. I join with my fellow librarians in wishing you success as head of our greatest library. I am sure that you have already learned that your task is primarily an administrative one; you must work with librarians and (let me whisper it) with the Congress and only indirectly with books.

It is a pleasure and an honor for me to introduce the Librarian of Congress who will give us the sixth and last of the Libraries and the Life of the Mind in America series with the title "The Indivisible Community." Dr. Daniel J. Boorstin.

Daniel J. Boorstin

Thank you, Dr. Metcalf. I want to thank all of you for that warm and generous welcome. And I especially want to thank Dr. Metcalf for reminding me and reminding all of us of the great tradition of the Library of Congress, and of the talents of my predecessors as Librarians of Congress. I am, of course, again reminded of my inadequacies to that job. I thought I had recognized most of them, but Dr. Metcalf has mentioned some others. Now I can add to my other disqualifications the fact that I was not born west of the Mississippi, and that I am not a poet.

The Library of Congress offers the greatest challenge that can be given to any thinking person—any person interested in the mind—and I'm grateful for the opportunity to do what I can there.

I would like first to make a couple of personal comments. I cannot speak on this occasion without first paying tribute to Allie Beth Martin, the librarian of the Tulsa County Library. That library was one of my earliest ties to the library profession. I remember well my father—many years ago—having worked to help organize the Tulsa County Library and to provide something better than the little Carnegie building that the public library had been housed in. So I am particularly aware of the great contribution that Allie Beth made, in giving Tulsa a modern and effective and growing library. We'll all miss her.

I would also like to mention just briefly a contribution which we at the Library of Congress want to make to this Centennial celebration of the American Library Association. On the 21st of September, the anniversary of the day when Thomas Jefferson offered his library to the United States, we will rechristen the second Library of Congress building. That building, formerly known as the Annex, now, by Act of Congress, has been named the Thomas Jefferson Building. We are doing this to celebrate the Centennial of the American Library Association, and to remind everyone of Jefferson's great contribution to the Library of Congress and to the profession of librarianship. He is our founding librarian. I hope that many of you will join us in Washington on the 21st of September. The American Library Association will have the central role and will be represented by Bob Wedgworth, your president, and others.

This has been a delightful occasion for Ruth and me—I don't know how we can thank you for the warmth of the reception. I would be less than honest if I didn't confess and—in the liberalism of our times—I think I might put it this way: This is a virginal occasion for me. It is my first attendance at a meeting of the American Library Association. Like all virginal occasions, it has offered a great deal of charm and a great deal of suspense—and, also, a few fears.

Since I have only been Librarian of Congress for so short a time, and since I still have so much to learn, this afternoon I will speak mainly as a historian. I will try to put the present state of American public libraries in perspective.

Some of the peculiar problems of public libraries nowadays, as well as my own situation, can be symbolized by an episode which occurs near the beginning of F. Scott Fitzgerald's novel *The Great Gatsby*. Two characters meet at a party. One observes, "I've been drunk for about a week now, and I thought it might sober me up to sit in a library." "Has it?" asks the other character, who has just walked into the library. The response is—and I think I perhaps would be willing to echo it—"A little bit I think, I can't tell yet. I've only been here an hour."

It is now a pleasure for me to offer the talk which I prepared as a historian in my study at home, on my own time, and without assistance from library personnel. This is part of the lecture series Libraries and the Life of the Mind.

THE INDIVISIBLE COMMUNITY

*T*HE PUBLIC LIBRARIES in our time are in limbo. In recent decades they have been in limbo—in two dictionary senses. First, limbo as we all know is a region or condition of oblivion or neglect; and it is also an intermediate place or state. Our public libraries are on the way to becoming our forgotten institution—a condition which has come about during the last few decades—despite the valiant efforts of my predecessors in the Library of Congress, despite the admirable corporate work of this Association, and despite the personal talents and energy of all of you.

I will try to suggest some of the historical explanation for the present situation. I would offer, as a couple of pieces of evidence, first, some of the observations and pictures in that delightful book by ALA's Art Plotnik. I am sure many of you have read *Library Life—American Style,* just published last year. The frontispiece, as you will recall, shows the attractive children's librarian for San Mateo County, California, helping two young Californians test the paper birds that they had made in the origami class at the El Granada branch. This suggests the remarkably novel outreach of the roles of libraries in our time. And another clue which might seem less obvious, but which I found rather shocking, is to be found in the *Historical Statistics of the United States* (Bicentennial Edition), which has just been published in two volumes by the Bureau of the Census of the United States Department of Commerce.

In these volumes you will find figures on all sorts of institutions and activities, including the sponge sales in Tarpon Springs, Florida, between 1913 and 1970, but you will not find statistics on libraries. Librarians are listed as part of the labor force, which I suppose is meant to be a compliment. And the only aspect of library budgets mentioned is that of the library budgets of institutions of higher learning. There are no statistics on libraries in general nor on public libraries. The last time that the *Historical Statistics of the United States* had such figures was in the 1949 edition.

Here are two clues to what I mean when I say our public libraries are in limbo. Our public libraries have moved into novel, intermediate roles, and they have come to suffer from oblivion or neglect. The situation is very different from that when this Association was founded almost one hundred years ago—in early October in Philadelphia at the Centennial Exposition of 1876.

The founding of this Association marked what I would call the first hey-day of American libraries. The great American library movement took its momentum from three founding principles. The great motive desires in those days were: first, self-help; second, autonomy of the individual; and third, community. These are three of the great founding principles of American civilization.

I would like briefly to suggest how these principles served the library movement and fulfilled the library movement and then, how the tendencies of history and the drift and momentum of technology have tended to blur or hinder these principles. The great forces at work—and which I will describe—are those which have made ours the Age of Broadcasting.

During the age when the American Library Association came into being there was a great enthusiasm for libraries. It was an age dominated by a democratic ideal, the ideal of spreading knowledge to all. It began, of course, in this country with the celebrated founding of the Boston Public Library in 1854, but that enthusiasm was world-wide. It had been expressed in the Ewart Act in England in 1850 and was articulated in the eloquence of all the great literary figures of the time. Charles Dickens, for example, at the epochal opening of the new library in Manchester, in 1852, called the library "a great free school, bent on carrying instruction to the poorest hearths." When William Makepeace Thackeray, also present on that occasion, saw ahead (in his own words) "the vista of popular libraries being established all over the country, and the educational and elevating influences which would necessarily flow from the extension of the movement," he was so overcome by emotion at that prospect that he had to sit down in the middle of his speech.

In the United States about 1875 there were some 188 public libraries in 11 states. By the turn of the century, the accomplishments of the library movement justified President Theodore Roosevelt's familiar observation (in his annual message to Congress, December 3, 1901) that the modern public library movement was "the most characteristic educational movement of the past 50 years." On that occasion he also described the Library of Congress as "the one National Library in the United States . . . housed in a building which is the largest and most magnificent yet erected for library uses." President Roosevelt said he hoped that the resources to be provided by Congress would enable the Library of Congress "to become not merely a center of research, but the chief factor in great cooperative efforts for the diffusion of knowledge and the advancement of learning."

I will remind you of some other signs of the prosperity and enthusiasms and energy of the library movement in those early years of the American Library Association. In 1870 the Library of Congress had become a copyright deposit library. In 1876 appeared the first edition of Dewey's classification system. We sometimes forget that Melvil Dewey made his great invention when he was only 25 years old. But we must not let his precocity discourage any of us. In 1887 Melvil Dewey founded his School of Library Economy at Columbia, where he took the then-bold step of admitting women.

Between 1874 and 1882 Charles Ammi Cutter's catalog of the Library of the Boston Athenaeum appeared, providing an elementary treatise in a pioneer area. From 1886 to 1919 the great Carnegie gifts were made which came to $40,000,000 for 1,679 public libraries in 1,412 communities. These gifts were probably the most economical and productive educational expenditures in all American history.

The Library of Congress played a leading role in this grand movement. In 1897 the Library of Congress classification system was developed. In 1901 Herbert Putnam began selling library cards. These became a national—even an international—symbol of librarians' solidarity. Today, in our world where nations seem able to agree on almost nothing else, it remains a cheering omen that they do seem to be able to agree upon the size of library cards—and the width of motion picture film. Of course, the Library of Congress had a great deal to do with creating that symbol.

That was an age of library enthusiasms. If you will look at any dictionary of quotations of the period, you will be impressed by the fact that there was hardly a great wit or a pundit of the age who didn't have something complimentary and high flown to say about libraries. The most famous of them perhaps was Thomas Carlyle's observation that "the true university of these days is a collection of books."

It was part of the general enthusiasm for spreading knowledge. It was part of the reform movement. We forget how widespread were its expressions. If you will read some of the correspondence between the applicants for Carnegie buildings and the Carnegie Foundation, and especially with John Bartram, the man who answered the correspondence for Andrew Carnegie, you will be shocked to see that the money was not awarded for a "building," but for a "bilding." Andrew Carnegie was an enthusiast for spelling reform. So, too, was Melvil Dewey, who also was an enthusiast for the metric system. And these are minor clues to the reformist spirit of the age.

In 1894, when Charles Ammi Cutter ended his first career at the Boston Athenaeum, he went to Northampton, Massachusetts, and made a new career of developing the Forbes Library. In a pioneer manifesto, he said that his hope there would be to shape "a new type of public library, which, speaking broadly, will lend everything to anybody in any desired quantity for any desired time." This was the product of his decades of experience as a pioneering librarian.

Generally speaking, public funds and government support did not match popular enthusiasm. The Library of Congress was an exception. For the Library of Congress has always been blessed by practical purposes. The universal benefits of these emphatically practical—legislative—purposes are not always universally understood in the library profession. We are, as our name wholesomely reminds us, the Library of *Congress*. One of the great features of our Library of Congress is that it has been a branch of Congressional good housekeeping. And we hope, of course, that it will remain effective both as the Congress' library and as the nation's library.

There were land grant colleges and there were land grant universities, but—and this is something that we don't see often enough observed—there were no land grant libraries. Of course many library institutions benefited indirectly from the founding of universities—and there were a few men of exceptional vision who gave fortunes for the express and primary purpose of founding libraries. We still profit from their beneficence at the Newberry Library in Chicago and the Huntington Library in San Marino, and there are others. But the great age of college founding (made possible by the fortunes of a Matthew Vassar, a Johns Hopkins, a Leland Stanford, and a John D. Rockefeller) was not matched by a great age of endowed library founding.

It is worth noting, incidentally, that the G.I. Bill after World War II, which brought millions in tuition fees to colleges and universities, gave no comparable direct support to libraries.

The limbo in which public libraries were to find themselves was to be explained also in part by certain traditional peculiarities of the library—and especially the American library—as an institution. I would like to remind you of these briefly.

First, there were conflicts of purpose. The first conflict was between the motive of preservation and the motive of diffusion. The problem was summed up in a statement by one of Bodley's early librarians, who observed that it was his job to protect the books from the public. But many people observed the cemetery-like quality of libraries and some cynics were fond of referring to libraries as places where ideas die. The popular preacher Henry Ward Beecher called the library "the soul's burial ground . . . the land of shadows." Macaulay, in his essay on Milton, you may recall, referred to "the dust and silence of the upper shelf."

In the early public libraries, too, there was much concern over the demeanor and dress of users. "The laboring classes" were thought to be people who might soil the books—and who were unlikely to show books the respect that they were entitled to. This created a conflict between the purpose of diffusion and the purpose of preservation.

There was another conflict of purpose. That was the conflict between the purpose of instruction, or uplift, and the purpose of entertainment. It was embodied in the dispute which I'm sure many of you know, between George Ticknor and his colleague Edward Everett over the proper kinds of books to be included in the Boston Public Library. How popular should the books be? Would you corrupt the taste of young men and women if you let them read books just for entertainment?

This particular conflict was symbolized in the contradictory kinds of appeals that went to Andrew Carnegie in asking for his benefaction. The officers of the Commercial Club in Bloomfield, Iowa, in 1911 appealed for a Carnegie gift for a public library because, they said, they were such a virtuous town. The town had not had a single saloon in thirty years. On the other hand, the mayor of Berlin, Wisconsin, in 1902 argued that their town ought to have a public library—in fact needed one more than most others—because in that town there were more than twenty saloons, and there was not one place where a young man could spend his evenings away from the influence of liquor.

This, of course, remains an issue: between uplift or instruction on the one hand and entertainment on the other. It is an issue that becomes increasingly blurred in our Age of Broadcasting.

Another problem of libraries has been that they have tended to be indirect or secondary service institutions. Our Library of Congress is a good example. The Library of Congress was founded primarily in the first instance to serve the Congress, and to help the Congress make more enlightened legislation. For many years the community as a whole was to be benefited by the library only through the improved quality of the works of the lawmakers. The best colonial libraries that were not in the hands of private individuals were also secondary in their services to the general public. The great Harvard College library, for example, was intended to serve the whole community, but only through its service to the select few fortunate enough to be students or faculty at Harvard. The *Historical Statistics of the United States* (Bicentennial Edition) which I mentioned earlier and which offers figures not on public libraries but on the libraries of colleges and universities bears witness to an enduring, misleading, emphasis on libraries as secondary services. Libraries are commonly considered to be institutions designed to serve some other institution.

Nowadays, we find this dramatized in a new way. Our preoccupation with the decay of cities and with multiplying urban problems has tempted politicians—and even "concerned citizens"—to treat public libraries as simply another "municipal service." Like the water supply, the garbage collection arrangements, or the sewerage system, a public library "system" is thought of not as serving people, but as serving "municipalities."

All this has tended to confuse and to bury the identity of the public library. Which has produced another too little-noticed problem. Libraries do not have organized alumni. It is, of course, debatable whether this is entirely a disadvantage, whether it would be an advantage to us to have a football team of the New York Public Library playing against the Detroit Public Library. But, at the same time, our libraries have suffered and lagged behind other educational and public institutions, and partly for this reason. The history of colleges and universities shows how many of their benefactions have come from grateful and also, sometimes, sentimental alumni.

Where are the library alumni? They're everywhere. And they include some of the most successful, most prosperous, and most public-spirited citizens. But the nature of the public library has left them anonymous, invisible, and unenlisted. We don't find people wearing rings certifying that they are a graduate of the Cleveland Public Library. Nor do they attend reunions to increase their hilarity and their devotion.

Students of American history are familiar with Sibley's classic fourteen-volume *Biographical Sketches of Those Who Attended Harvard College,* with Dexter's six volumes on Yale graduates, and with similar works on every major college or university—which all celebrate and advertise their educational achievement. But we have no comparable works on the "graduates" of our great libraries!

Self-made men or men "self-made" with the aid of public libraries, when successful, tend to give their fortunes to colleges and universities. There are some exceptions, but they are relatively few. Libraries generally receive only the crumbs. And this, too, helps us understand why libraries have been in limbo. They lack an impressive and vivid and familiar corporate identity. While people think of a college as an institution, they tend to think of a public library as a building.

We can, I think, revive the spirit and the motives of the founding era. We can bring our libraries out of limbo, if we will recall the importance of those three principled motives which I mentioned a few minutes ago—self-help, autonomy, and community—and if we succeed in finding special ways to fulfill those purposes in our time.

Now we live in a new era. It is the age not of democratizing knowledge, but the age of democratizing experience. We could sum it up by calling it the Age of Broadcasting.

This Age of Broadcasting is radically different from the previous age, and the novelty can be suggested by the new meaning of the word "broadcast." That word came into our language originally through the usages of agriculture and through Arthur Young's writings on farming. "Broadcast" as an adjective first meant "scattered abroad"—that is, scattered over the whole surface of the soil instead of being sowed in drills or rows.

"Broadcast" entered our language in a new sense in 1922 when radio made it possible to scatter messages in a new way, without regard to roads or walls; scattered abroad by the wireless telegraphy was the meaning which then came in.

One of the special features, revolutionary features, of this new kind of diffusion was that now messages were to be scattered in a new sense. They were sent out to anonymous, undetermined, even indeterminate, audiences. You might still know who was sending the message, but there was a new mystery—who was listening?

How much were they listening to? And how seriously were they listening? This new mystery then created a new science, the science of market research—and a science which has not yet unraveled all of the mystery by any means.

Coincidentally with this and as a result of the same technology which made it possible to broadcast, it became possible to spread abroad a whole new set of sensations. What was spread about now was not what was spread in the previous Age of Publishing. Technology had changed and enlarged what could be diffused. In this new era what was diffused was not merely the familiar old product—the printed written word or the graven image—not merely the translation of experience by an author or an artist, but the very sensations of experience.

Living sounds. Living voices. Moving living images. In living color. What was diffused was not just knowledge but *experience*. Experience of distant places, great events, people in high stations. What were some of the new consequences of this for the spreading of other kinds of messages —those which we have in our charge?

In the first place, now messages were taken to the people. Formerly, people had to go after the messages. The motive of self-help was partly removed. Now people could simply sit there—at home, or wherever else they happened to be—and get the message.

Second, it became an age of networks and channels. This was to be an age of the decline of choice, the decline of autonomy.

And finally, and this will be most important for us who want to promote the public library movement, it was an age of the decline of community. People now found it less necessary to congregate—to come together in the visible presence of other human beings. Community was attenuated as people were segregated into their own living rooms. The paradox was that there was to be a strange communalizing of experience and vivifying of experience along with this new segregation of individuals.

This democratizing of experience came as the climax of one of the most rapid and most remarkable revolutions in history. We have lived through a cataclysm of technology. And most of this has come in the century since the American Library Association was founded.

It was a coincidence, but there was deep symbolic significance in the fact that the Philadelphia exposition of 1876, the occasion when the American Library Association was founded, was also the first grand national exhibit of the marvels of technology. That was the occasion of the successful demonstration of Alexander Graham Bell's telephone, which was itself a clue to the electronic roots of many new problems. The technological momentum of the new age was signaled by the development of the phonograph, built by Thomas A. Edison in 1877, by the incandescent lamp which he made commercially practicable in 1879, and by the rise of the photograph, which was announced when the first popular camera was patented by George Eastman under the name of Kodak in 1888. Celluloid, which proved essential to the development of movies, was patented by Edison in 1888. Radio came by 1920 when David Sarnoff was marketing his radio music boxes.

And then of course, the climax—television—whose arrival in our time I remember vividly. The first commercial TV broadcasting stations appeared in the United States in 1941, when there were two. Seven years later, in 1948, there were 108 stations and a million sets. By 1970 over 95 percent of American households had television.

The consequences of this in democratizing experience were overwhelming. The result—so commonplace that we do not even realize it—has been to change the very nature of time and space. Now you're more there when you're here than when you're there.

The tendency of this Age of Broadcasting, moreover, is to broadcast everything. Even the mails—that formerly were a means of complimenting people by addressing messages to them personally—became addressed to that universal, anonymous, irritating destination—"Occupant." Junk mail is nothing but broadcasting by nonelectronic means. It is a way of spreading something abroad without regard to whether the person who receives it wants it or needs it.

Even book publishing, increasingly dominated by the market for paperbacks, has tended to become a kind of broadcasting. Paperback books are marketed by being "scattered over the whole surface" of the market. They are not destined for particular purchasers but spread abroad in the hope that somebody—anybody—will pick them up. As paperback publishers remind us, perhaps the most important feature of a paperback is the jacket design. Paperbacks are marketed on newsstands and in airport kiosks where they compete with magazines, candy bars, and other items bought on impulse. One of the most successful publishers of paperback books reports that items that have not already shown their impulse appeal in these markets are expected to be returned after nine days.

Libraries, we hope, can provide us an escape from the limitations of this broadcast world. But here we must be wary of falling into a common fallacy in the interpretation of history. This is what I call the Displacive Fallacy.

We are tempted to think—and this may be due in part to our excessive faith in technology—that, just as a victorious army defeats its enemies, so the new technology conquers the old technology. It is easy to find examples of mistaken prophecies based on the Displacive Fallacy. For example, there were confident predictions that the telephone would abolish the mail. There were firm predictions that the radio would make the telephone obsolete. That the phonograph would be the end of live concerts. That television would be the end of radio. Then, of course, that television would abolish the book. And now, that the computer will displace humankind.

All these predictions were based on a misconception. Shall we say a teleological misconception? A misconception about the purpose or end for which people invent technology and develop their institutions. It is a misconception which is quite un-American. For it rests on the notion that technology is simply a way to satisfy fixed needs. If you satisfy the needs in one way, then you won't have to satisfy them in another way. The history of technology and of institutions is not, however, the story of "instead." It is the story of "also." Experience is not substitutive, but additive and cumulative. The American experience—the very existence of American experience, on this, the most unnecessary of all continents—proved that human needs and wants can be ever-expanding. The great inventors do not merely satisfy needs, they invent needs. This is what I call the Exploring Spirit, which I describe in my little volume of that title (Random House, 1976).

Printed books were among the first great stirrers of the Exploring Spirit. They created and awakened a vast range of unimagined wants and needs. Who wanted an automobile? What people wanted was a better horse or a better carriage. Henry Ford not only invented a new means of transportation; it would be most misleading to put it that way. He invented a new need. The automobile. Then came television. And now, of course, the computer, which reaches farther out beyond the imagined needs of scholars than any of its predecessors.

The new technology, then, has not abolished libraries or the book and never will. But it has created new roles for books and for libraries. Libraries can provide escapes from the new limitations of our Age of Broadcasting. First, I will suggest some of the new opportunities that our age has provided for the book and for libraries. These arise out of the very peculiarities of our novel ways of democratizing experience. Then I will suggest some of the ways in which we as librarians may make wider and more effective use of the characteristic products of the Age of Broadcasting toward our more traditional purposes.

In the first place, the library has a new opportunity to promote the motive and the desire for self-help. It is an antidote for the declining sense of skill. The TV audience is skill-less and only half-attentive. TV-land, a supremely democratic land where all can enter free of charge, is a world where no skill is required as a passport. There are few levels of TV-viewing. Anybody can get something from watching a tennis match or "All in the Family." Only a few can get anything from reading Kant or Proust or Joyce. While reading is graded, television-viewing can only be restricted. What is X-rated is not so rated because it's hard to understand, but because it's too easy to understand.

In the world of books, by contrast, your skill increases your reach. Printing, once called the *ars artium omnium conservatrix*, might now also be called the art stimulative of all the arts.

Now libraries are needed as the antidote to the undifferentiated audience—and to preserve the motive of autonomy by encouraging the individual and conserving the small group with a specialized interest. Television has a congenital emphasis on entertainment, because entertainment is an activity with the most undifferentiated appeals. "Educational television" nowadays is presented as if it were some startling innovation. But there have been educational books for centuries.

The book has long since offered in high degree the special individualized virtues of cable television. Every book ultimately is aimed at an audience of one. A book can be published without even being assigned a channel. The publisher need not produce any certain amount of religious matter, need not advertise the community activities. He can even suggest the benefits of smoking or of any activity which is beginning to be unrespectable in the community as a whole. Libraries, moreover, are a natural antidote everywhere to the perils of the government-controlled broadcasting channel. We librarians are the natural conservers and promoters of free communication.

While publishing in the United States has moved farther and farther away from censorship, broadcasting even in our free country has come increasingly under government scrutiny, and is likely to become ever more so. As TV-land finds it ever harder to be, the world of the book is the land of the free and the home of the brave.

The library is an antidote—ever more needed in the Age of Broadcasting—to patron control. While we think of television as our most modern medium, in one crucial respect television has stayed back in the eighteenth century. About that time the book began to escape from the dominance of rich and powerful patrons. But broadcasting still remains in the Age of the Patron.

The broadcasting audience can respond only indirectly to what the patron provides on the airwaves—by buying or not buying the product. In the world of the book, however, the reader and the buyer remain sovereign.

Finally, the library can be an avenue into the whole human community. It can be a corrective to TV-myopia—the myopia which enlarges out of all proportion our sense of the contemporary, which widens and shortens our vision of the chronological foreground. That myopia makes it difficult for us to see what extends back beyond the age of photography.

The great electronic conqueror of space cannot conquer time. Only the book—and the other media that we have at our disposal—can accomplish that. Books remain our messengers from the longer past and to the longer future.

Books remain, and libraries remain, our symbols of community with all humankind. With the world-wide rise and multiplication of chauvinisms, the library and the book remain our escape from the prison of the present and from the provincialism of our nation's confines.

These are some of the ways in which the peculiar limitations of broadcasting have given new roles to books and to libraries. But the new technology of the Age of Broadcasting itself offers us new opportunities. In conclusion I will briefly suggest some of these.

Radio and television are not enemies of the book. They can be new allies of the book. We must recognize and enlist our new allies. They can help us in our mission of the diffusion of knowledge and the advancement of learning. We must find ways to make television our ally, to make it the trailer and the appetizer for the library and the whole world of books.

Television channels, which must justify themselves for their public service, announce freely and frequently the time, the weather, the news, the latest catastrophe and the next television program (which sometimes ought to be classified in that category). It's astonishing—it's even shocking—to me that our conscience-flaunting television networks have taken so little responsibility for leading viewers from the television screens into the wider world of books that is always waiting. We, as book people and as librarians, must see that that's changed. Of course, we occasionally see the announcement of the names of printed matter and books in book-review programs and book-discussion programs. But these are generally aimed at small audiences and seldom appear on the commercial networks. Generally when we see a book listed, it is in the credits for a television program. When we are simply told the name of a book that a program has been adapted from, we often conclude that now we needn't bother to read the book, since we've seen the television program instead.

But that situation need not remain. Recently at a convention of the Association of American Publishers, I suggested that we seek new ways to use television to make TV-viewers into more avid book readers and more enthusiastic library users. The book publishers, who are already undertaking an imaginative program to use television during the coming Christmas season to persuade more TV-viewers to become book buyers, greeted my suggestion with enthusiasm. They will cooperate in our efforts as librarians to improve the reading habits and widen and deepen the literacy of our nation of TV audiences. We have a hint of how far we still have to go, and how much persuading we still need to do, in the fact that the leading "cultural" correspondent of our leading national newspaper snidely reported my suggestion as the kind of thinking that had brought the dinosaur to his doom. But we must and can and will find ways to enlarge contemporary literacy. We will use the television screen itself to alert people to the wealth that awaits them in libraries and the whole world of books.

We must find ways, moreover, to give to our library users wider choices not only in the world of books, but in all the other means of democratizing experience. Of course, most of our libraries are already offering these choices, but we should do even more—to offer the increasing product of sound and sight recording.

We must find ways to use our technology (certainly the computer, but not only the computer) to help us develop networks which will enable us to share our resources. All this will help us accomplish the purpose which Josiah Quincy described in 1841 (the hope of those who were trying to found a Boston Public Library), "to give the intellectual treasures of the civilized world the same dissemination and equalization which commerce [had] already given to its material ones."

Just as the Library of Congress, inspired by that great librarian Herbert Putnam, has advanced in the past three-quarters of a century from the centrally prepared library card and interlibrary loans into countless other ways of sharing, so now the computer can open a new era of collaboration and shared resources. The computer enables us in new and startling ways to repeal the traditional laws of physics, which once declared that anything can be in only one place at a time.

The Age of Broadcasting calls for a library renaissance. There is an unprecedented need for the unique resources of the book. At the same time there are crushing new pressures which disintegrate and discourage the grand improving motives of self-help, autonomy, and community. But there are vast new resources which we can use to nourish these very motives, to encourage them, and to give them a justified sense of fulfillment. Libraries remain the meccas of self-help. They remain as they have always been, the most open of open universities—institutions of the highest learning, where there are no entrance examinations, no registration fees, no examinations, and no diplomas, and where one can enter at any age. There we make available the great teachers of all ages and all nations. We have no problem with tenure. In this invisible endless faculty of great teachers, they all have tenure, and yet none of them becomes senile or lazy, nor can they inhibit their successors. And we need not worry that any of them will be distracted from their teaching.

We have no problems there of "publish or perish," for there the published never perishes. As librarians we share the mission of the greatest teachers: To help others help themselves. This is what we mean by autonomy, independence, self-government—the ideals of a democratic people. Libraries remain islands of choice in a world of channels.

In this supermarket of ideas and arts, every citizen can choose his nourishment from the products old and new, of the whole human race. Ours is a workshop of do-it-yourself programming, where no citizen need wait for a national broadcast or even a local station.

The library is par excellence a place of community, for there we share the spiritual wealth of all humankind. We must find ways to enlist the material wealth of our nation—at all levels, federal, state, and local—to accomplish and fulfill this community. In the United States, of all places, our library institutions are products of community, mostly local communities.

We must strengthen our libraries as communities of the Exploring Spirit. Places where people are stirred to ask questions they never imagined from people they never knew. Where people are enticed into the adventures of the unexpected, the unknown, and the unimagined. Where we nourish creative dissatisfaction, where the human hunger for knowledge and the appetite for enlarging experience are stirred in the very act of searching.

We librarians must explore together in our search for new worlds of autonomy, self-help, and community. The Library of Congress pledges its friendly fellowship in this common adventure, an adventure which brings us out of limbo and which will fulfill our special American vision of a community of communities.